To My Dearest F

I trust you will be my number one fan.

Best Wishes
Asmin Jahan
(your 'batiji')

THE ROOT OF ALL EVIL

THE ROOT OF ALL EVIL

Tasmin Jahan

The Book Guild Ltd
Sussex, England

First published in Great Britain in 2004 by
The Book Guild Ltd,
25 High Street,
Lewes, East Sussex
BN7 2LU

Copyright © Tasmin Jahan 2004

The right of Tasmin Jahan to be identified as the author of this work has
been asserted by her in accordance with the
Copyright, Designs and Patents Act 1988.

All rights reserved. No part of this publication may be reproduced,
transmitted, or stored in a retrieval system, in any form or by any means,
without permission in writing from the publisher, nor be
otherwise circulated in any form of binding or cover other than that in
which it is published and without a similar condition being imposed on
the subsequent purchaser.

Typesetting in Times by
IML Typographers, Birkenhead, Merseyside

Printed in Great Britain by
Antony Rowe Ltd, Chippenham, Wiltshire

A catalogue record for this book is
available from The British Library

ISBN 1 85776 836 1

*Think of one day –
Think of your worst enemy –
Think of your family –
Think who could it be?*

THE ROOT OF ALL EVIL
***
DRAMATIS PERSONAE

Main Characters

Frederick Devereux – head of the family

Veronica Devereux – his second wife (Loni Devereux was his first wife)

Sophie Devereux – his sister

Thomas Devereux – his elder son

Nancy Devereux – his elder daughter

Penelope Devereux – his younger daughter

Benjamin Devereux – his younger son

Mansion Staff

Penchard – Frederick Devereux's personal assistant

Rose – the cook

Peter – the under-butler

Coral – principal maid

Meesha – secondary maid

Patrick – the gardener

Additional Characters

Jim and Raisor – local thugs

John Braswick – Devereux factory employee

Josie McIntyre – Thomas's girlfriend

Daniel Sullivan – Penelope's estranged husband

Mishty Shakar – Nancy's friend

Samuel Calcott – the journalist

Jack Haddy – organiser of the Devereux Extravaganza

Estonia Darvel – guest at the Devereux Extravaganza

Frank Molloy – second guest at the Devereux Extravaganza

SCENE ONE

Fezaria-Aston, a picturesque and serene Kentish town. It is a dark and cold night. Two ruffians, Jim and Raisor, appear. They seem rather filthy and creepy. A cadaver is sprawled in front of them. Jim is kneeling down, holding a pale hand, whilst Raisor is standing beside him.

RAISOR: Can you find her pulse? Jim, can you find her pulse?
JIM: I'm trying, I'm trying.
RAISOR: This is all your fault, you know.
JIM: Will you please shut up, Raisor!
RAISOR: All we were supposed to do was scare her. After all, she's only a woman. And women scare easy.
JIM: I know what was supposed to happen.
RAISOR: Mr Devereux is going to go ballistic! Do you think he'll pay us after this?
JIM: Maybe.
RAISOR: Have you found it?
JIM: Will you stop?
RAISOR: Let me try.
JIM: No. I can manage.
RAISOR: She looks really dead, you know. She looks really pale. She could have fainted, you know.
JIM: But she didn't.
RAISOR: The shovel must have really hurt.
JIM: That was the whole idea.
RAISOR: She's quite nice, isn't she? Beneath that pale look she seems rather peaceful, don't you think? As if she's in deep thought about something. What are we going to do if she doesn't wake up?

JIM: Drag her body to Monument Valley and hide it.
RAISOR: What about Mr Devereux? What are we going to tell him?
JIM: We'll have to tell him the truth.
RAISOR: But we're not used to telling the truth.
JIM: We killed her by accident. We didn't do it on purpose.
RAISOR: Mr Devereux is going to torture us, I just know it. I never wanted to die young. Do you think he'll give us a last wish?
JIM: Raisor, please put a cork in it! Someone might hear you.
RAISOR: My last wish would be to see Mexico. That would be my dream come true. Me and the chicas and the big fat hats and my bottle of whisky. After that, I don't mind dying.
JIM: (*sarcastically*)   What a wonderful vision! Why don't you ask Mr Devereux if he'll pay for a ticket and send you there?
RAISOR: Yeah, I could, but you know what? I don't like aeroplanes. There's nothing to support them in the sky, you know. I'd hate to fall down and hurt myself.
JIM: Raisor, planes have engines so that they can stay in the air for a very long time.
RAISOR: Yeah, I know that, but Jedd was telling me there are long pieces of invisible string holding it up the whole way to Mexico. If one snaps, it will start to wobble and then you begin to float like a fish until you end up on top of someone.
JIM: Raisor, you know how I always tell you, you're really stupid and strange?
RAISOR: Yeah?
JIM: You still bloody are. Jedd was winding you up. Planes and strings? What a load of nonsense! Now will you shut up and let me finish the job!
RAISOR: Well, for your information, my mum doesn't think I'm stupid or strange. She thinks I'm beautiful.
JIM: We are doing an important thing here. Will you stop harping on about rubbish and stick to the job?

RAISOR: One of these days I'm going to say something so important that none of you will be listening!
JIM: Now, judging by the standard of this work, I think Mr Devereux will just ruin our chances of getting any other jobs. He won't be severe.
RAISOR: What if he cuts off all our links? What if we starve to death?
JIM: We won't starve to death, you fool! We've got my uncle's farm, haven't we?
RAISOR: Maybe we should really lie?
JIM: (*sarcastically*) Maybe we should leave town?
RAISOR: Good idea!
JIM: Oh, stop being so stupid. All we have to do is be up front about it and then we'll see what happens. If we have to leave town then we will organise something.
RAISOR: Are you sure you didn't find her pulse?
JIM: Raisor, she's dead. We killed her. Good and proper.
RAISOR: So she's not coming back!
JIM: No.
RAISOR: Oops!
JIM: We better take her to Monument Valley then. Come on.
RAISOR: Jim, everything will be all right, won't it?
JIM: Of course. We're in this together. And in any case, maybe this happened for the best.
RAISOR: Hope Mr Devereux thinks so! You know I did have a funny feeling about this job. This morning when I was trying to have breakfast I found myself just staring at it. I couldn't put it in my mouth. My stomach was churning and crying out so much. It was as if somebody had tied a knot in my throat.
JIM: You grab her legs and I'll grab her arms.
RAISOR: You reckon she's got any money on her?
JIM: No. I already checked.
RAISOR: Apple pie?
JIM: What?

RAISOR: I really fancy some apple pie. I like it when the warm juicy apple bits melt in my mouth, you know. What about cigarettes?
JIM: She doesn't look the smoking type. Her fingers aren't stained and her teeth are very clean.
RAISOR: Shame. I could really do with a puff.

The two men prepare to lift the body, JIM *standing behind the girl's head,* RAISOR *taking up a position at her feet.*

RAISOR: What do you think her dying wish would have been, you know, if she knew she was going to die?
JIM: Since when did we care?
RAISOR: Oh, she's so young and pretty. I bet she looks pretty in pink. I bet she has a handsome boyfriend who really loves her and misses her when she's not there. If her boyfriend knew about this I bet he would rush to be at her side, hold her very close to him, look into her lovely eyes and kiss her so gently until her soul is no longer at one with his.
JIM: Have you finished, Dr Love? Now can we get on with it?
RAISOR: Well, as her boyfriend isn't here, shall I kiss her?
JIM: Not only are you stupid and strange, but you're really disgusting. Why do you want to kiss a dead girl?
RAISOR: That's not fair. I haven't kissed a woman in three years, and that was my mum!
JIM: Raisor, it's almost time for supper. We need to hurry.
RAISOR: Just one small kiss.
JIM: No! I'm not going to let you be disgusting in front of me! Raisor, she is dead. She's worm food now. You are not going to kiss worm food in front of me.
RAISOR: I wish some girl would fancy me. I have so many hopes, you know. Haven't been to the cinema for ages.
JIM: On a count of three, we're going to pick her up. Ready?
RAISOR: Maybe there's something wrong with me. That's why women don't look at me in a romantic way.

JIM: One...
RAISOR: Maybe it's the way I walk...
JIM: Two...
RAISOR: Or maybe it's my hair...
JIM: Three!

They lift the body together and begin to walk along slowly.

JIM: Blimey, she's quite heavy for a thin girl.
RAISOR: I just don't understand! It's not as if I'm looking for a relationship or any sort of commitment. I'm not even asking for an arm or a leg. I just want to do the tango lying down until I can't take any more. That's all!
JIM: Are you aware that you're actually still talking?
RAISOR: You're all right, you've got a wife and four kids and three sheep. I've got nothing. Just a small roof over my head, a sick mother and a ferocious donkey called Rambo.
JIM: Am I the only one holding her?
RAISOR: You won't even let me near your sister!
JIM: She doesn't like older men. And besides, she thinks you're ugly and you smell like a pig.
RAISOR: (*begins to get upset*) Well, some people are just into appearances, aren't they?
JIM: Will you keep your mind on the job? (*Pause.*) All right, all right. Out of our whole group, when you do make an effort, you are the one who's handsome, you're the one who's very fashionable, very kind, very thoughtful and very charming. You know what? Lucy, the tulip and lily girl down at Franco's Valley, was asking about you yesterday. Maybe you should meet her?
RAISOR: Really? You didn't tell me she had a thing for me.
JIM: Let's get to Monument Valley and we'll talk about it then.

RAISOR: How brilliant is that? Of course, I'm handsome. What was I thinking?

As they exit, carrying away the body, JIM *gives an exasperated look.*

SCENE TWO

The Devereux mansion. FREDERICK DEVEREUX *and his younger son are in the study.* MR DEVEREUX, *60 years of age, is a man of great opulence and superiority. He is the head of the Devereux family, tall, dark, of slim build, and has a striking moustache. He is making a drink. His son* BENJAMIN, *24 years old, is sitting at his father's desk. He is rather tall, fair, handsome and of medium build.*

BENJAMIN: You seem rather happy today, Father?
FREDERICK: I have cause to celebrate, my son. Would you like to join me for a drink?
BENJAMIN: Sure. Why not? Whatever you're having.
FREDERICK: This certainly marks the end of a contemptuous period.
BENJAMIN: Contemptuous? Father, what are you talking about?
FREDERICK: There was this awful constraint, this ugly head of poverty-stricken gunk within my realm that I had to crush. I thought I would take the matter slowly and then go in heavy-handed, but the buffoons accidentally went overboard and made that jubilant vision come true.
BENJAMIN: What buffoons?
FREDERICK: Benjamin, my dear son, I have been so worried about you. For the past few months things have been rather tense between us. We have been rude and unbelievably distant from one another. Your Auntie Sophie talked of living within a war zone. Now, for the first time, we can say goodbye to all that heartache and start afresh.
BENJAMIN: Father, are you talking about Michelle and I?

FREDERICK: Yes. The biggest and most distressing mismatch in the whole of Fezaria-Aston.
BENJAMIN: But I thought I had made my feelings absolutely clear about this? No matter what, I want to be with her! I've promised!
FREDERICK: As a father it is my responsibility to keep my family name – keep the Devereux name – always on the highest pillar possible. Nobody had the audacity to tarnish even a little bit of our reputation until you made your unfortunate announcement.
BENJAMIN: There is nothing wrong with Michelle.
FREDERICK: No, there never was. It is just that her background is appalling, her family name is muck and her standard of living bears similarity to that of our sick cows on the farm.
BENJAMIN: Father! I demand you to stop this kind of talk.
FREDERICK: I'm only saying it how it really is. We have built an enviable empire through years of blood and sweat. We deserve to have what we have. Nobody helped us. Nobody gave us any money. We had to start from scratch. Everything around you is all hard work. Just take a look. Who would not want to be in our shoes? Who would not want to indulge themselves like we do? And, my son, to explain this to you upsets me because not only are you enjoying the pleasures of other people's hard work, but you have never worked one whole day in your life! You can only define your loss if you have something like this to lose. I am always looking at a much larger picture than you. My gaze sees more facets than anybody else's in this mansion. You're simply thinking about yourself, whereas I am thinking of an entire generation.
BENJAMIN: Father, if I were to think about others, then where would I come into it? Who would consider my feelings? I thought you were a firm believer in 'every man for himself'?

FREDERICK: Your attitude, Benjamin, only shows self-centredness to me. You find the people around you, especially your own family, a great impediment. You cannot simply be a Devereux by name, you must act like one. After all these years, son, why do you not understand this?

BENJAMIN: I'm afraid, Father, I still stand by my decision. I want to marry Michelle. I want to be with her always. I find it totally unacceptable that everyone cannot grasp this notion. I wish to lead a happy and honest life with Michelle.

FREDERICK: Happiness and honesty? With a pauper?

BENJAMIN: I do realise that she is of very little status, but whatever the issue honesty is always the best policy.

FREDERICK: No it is not! Honesty never was the best policy. That proverb was only intended for those who had no money, no dignity and no suitable standard of living. Don't give me such shoddy talk. Honesty breeds objectionable implications. If we were always honest with each other, we would have more enemies, there would be no point in achieving our goals, there would be more suicides, and above all every person's weaknesses would be exposed.

BENJAMIN: I must say, Father, your definition is quite interesting.

FREDERICK: That's because I am right.

BENJAMIN: Well, Father, of all people I do not wish to make you my enemy, but if I am penalised for being honest then so be it. I have no other choice. Everybody must learn to accept my partner.

FREDERICK: You are asking for the impossible. You are preparing yourself to die like a hungry and foolish man. Do you know what it is to be hungry? You will only realise your mistake, as many people do, when it is too late.

BENJAMIN: Well, I sincerely hope that you are wrong.

FREDERICK: Benjamin, I am hardly in the wrong. You are rich. She is poor. She will use you until she has made use of every expedient practicable and then she will use her persuasive and undignified finesse to melt you down completely. Thus bringing you back to my doorstep a shattered and traumatised man.

BENJAMIN: You tell such a winding tale, Father.

FREDERICK: Poor means restriction. Poor is quite purely embarrassing. Without money you are nothing. Money gives you respect. Money gives you authority. It eases your mind and gives you freedom. With money you have choices. It lets you do whatever you want. Your idea of just being well educated and reeling off beliefs that you can make great things happen is only a youngster's myth. Knowledge merely gets you through a conversation. You are solely made the centre of attention for a few minutes. It does not make you wealthy. When you are affluent you do not have to say anything more than you need to. In some cases your money speaks volumes. (*He notices that* BENJAMIN *is not listening*) As my reprimand is falling on deaf ears, maybe your Auntie Sophie will have a better way of explaining the rest thoroughly.

BENJAMIN: The buffoons that you mentioned earlier. What did they do exactly?

FREDERICK: Without going into too much detail, they have made a significant transformation that will help heal a lot of damage caused during the past few months.

BENJAMIN: Surely you could explain a little more, Father. I am not one for cryptic talk.

FREDERICK: As I do not wish to ruin my new-found happiness, I shall leave it up to your Auntie to break the invigorating news. My temper is under control, Benjamin, and I really do not have the energy to bicker. My heart is not what it used to be.

BENJAMIN: Being your son is one of the hardest and most demanding roles I have ever had to fulfil. As each day goes by, I wonder whether you actually take great pleasure in mentally torturing me or is it something I am destined to face? You have no idea how tired and lonely I feel.

FREDERICK: It is called adulthood. You must learn to absorb how the system within this mansion works. Yes, you are my son, and, yes, you are next to my heart, but you are also a man who has a huge amount to achieve. Until you do so I have enormous difficulty in showing you pertinent respect and admiration. I certainly will not strangle my own morals for someone else. Hardly my cup of tea. Especially if the whole family name is in jeopardy. I know what I am doing and I fully comprehend what I am saying. If these words sound strenuous to your ears then please rest them for they will have to be wide open to those of your aunts.

BENJAMIN: As usual, Father, you're not being fair! Why are you weaving such a vicious circle?

FREDERICK: My responsibility as a father deems it necessary. Something you will only realise when you have a son of your own.

BENJAMIN: Pardon me for saying this, Father, but, quite frankly, I will be more supportive. I do not wish to follow in your footsteps.

Suddenly, the door opens with a bang. THOMAS DEVEREUX, *the elder son, enters. He is a little drunk. He is 33 years of age, quite tall, dark, slim and very good looking.*

THOMAS: Sorry to barge in like this, but could one of you lend me some money? I did have some before, but now I'm absolutely penniless. I must have spent it all.

FREDERICK: Thomas Devereux, do you have no control over your manners?

THOMAS: Look, Father, I need a drink. I need to feel good, so can I have some money or perhaps my inheritance?

FREDERICK: What inheritance?

THOMAS: Look, I just need enough so that I can pay for two rounds down at the Lion's Head. You should come with me, Father. We all have such a cracking time down there.

FREDERICK: Please leave before I call security.
BENJAMIN: Tom, here you go.

BENJAMIN *hands him some money.* THOMAS *grabs the notes and stuffs them in his pocket.*

THOMAS: You see, Father, this is called blood. You're not my relation at all, are you? You don't love me, but don't worry, I love you to bits. I love you for who you are. I don't care about your faults or your revulsion towards me. I love you dearly. Just like I love mummy dearly. I love you both. You know, we should all love each other. Amen!
FREDERICK: Please leave. I do not like talking to you when you are intoxicated.
THOMAS: I am not drunk! I'm perfectly sober! Look at these steady hands. I'm a steady person.
BENJAMIN: You'd better go now.
THOMAS: (*To his father*)   Why can't you accept me for who I am? It's not as if I'm sleeping with the maid or stealing money from the family safe? I haven't done anything wrong, Father.
FREDERICK: No of course you haven't, Thomas. The only major imperfection that did occur was thirty-three years ago when your mother decided to give birth to her impudent and vulgar son and then leave me with the depressing burden of nurturing you.
THOMAS: Well, I'm going to see my mother and ask her if she agrees with you or whether with disgust she is turning in her grave. At least, she'll listen to me, and she doesn't think I have a drinking problem.
FREDERICK: If you know what is best for you, you will get out of this room now!
THOMAS: You don't have to take that tone with me. I was leaving anyway. See you later, Ben. Oh, before I forget, I don't know if either of you have heard, Tunnell's bakery caught fire yesterday.

BENJAMIN: Really? How did that happen?
THOMAS: Well, truth be known, I was trying to do something and it went a little off beam, but don't tell anyone.
FREDERICK: Thomas, what were you attempting?
THOMAS: You promise you won't tell anyone?
FREDERICK: Thomas Devereux, please speak your mind!
THOMAS: I was trying to woo Josie McIntyre. She had put forty chelsea buns in the oven and had a few minutes to spare, so I thought, this is my chance. I was doing so well until this burning odour came wafting into the atmosphere and it completely ruined my power of love. As the blaze worsened I thought I might as well disappear, so I did.
BENJAMIN: What about Josie?
THOMAS: I don't know. I think she got away all right. I'll check if she's all right tomorrow. Now, I must have that drink.
FREDERICK: You fool! What on earth were you thinking? Do you have the slightest idea about the implications of your incessant stupidity?
THOMAS: Like I said, Father, I thought I really had a chance to bring out the hidden sparkle in her eyes and . . .
FREDERICK: Will you please refrain from all this nonsense at once! I do not wish to hear what you choose to do in your spare time. I suppose now I will be expecting Mr Tunnell. My son, the local Casanova-turned-arsonist. Laying out a costly path of trepidation for me. Surely the lock on your door has been fixed, Thomas? For goodness sake, why don't you use it! That way you will remain out of trouble and not cause so much misery.
THOMAS: Is it the money that is bothering you? If you pay for the damage now, I can guarantee you will be repaid. I will endeavour to find a job and I will work day and night until I have reimbursed you.
FREDERICK: Your life is within these four walls. Nobody will give you a job. Above all, nobody will deem you even fit to

make sense of any responsibility. You are simply an outcast within the Devereux clan. And why is that? Your interminable excuse being depression, which completely overrides any hope of accomplishment.

THOMAS: Wow. I must have been switched at birth because clearly if you were my father, you would speak with a much kinder tone and talk to me in a much gentler manner.

FREDERICK: This is all due to your juvenile behaviour, Thomas. If you were the least bit normal, I would appreciate that. You certainly would not witness this sort of discourse.

THOMAS: Oh, I'm bored. I must dash.

FREDERICK: Before you disappear, young man, there is something in particular that I would very much like to bring to your attention.

THOMAS: Is it going to be something exciting, like a surprise?

FREDERICK: If only it were. I have recent reports from a certain source that you were seen departing from the residence of Madame Lubelle. Is that correct?

THOMAS: Maybe.

FREDERIC: Thomas Devereux, please do not try my patience. Were you or were you not at that address some time last week?

THOMAS: Who gave you that information? Was it the inferior and brainless Penchard? He's a bit of a slimy rat, isn't he? I wish you wouldn't instruct him to follow me. You must be paying him a mountainous sum for such a dull and sluggish job. Anyway, who's to say he didn't go in there for his personal pleasure? Madame Lubelle does have quite an extended list of clientele. You would be amazed if you saw it.

FREDERICK: So you admit to it?

THOMAS: I am admitting to anything you want me to. Anything that makes you happy, Father. I cannot stand being in the same room as you with such irreconcilable differences between us!

FREDERICK: Your thought is hardly touching, Thomas. You

must refrain from visiting such undignified and low-class quarters. How dare you embarrass the family! I knew you had gone astray many years ago, but not so far as this.

THOMAS: It's just for mere company. You are mistaken if you believe that I go in there for something else!

FREDERICK: Company! Company! You have two sisters in this mansion. You have Benjamin, your Auntie Sophie and Veronica, not to forget Penchard! What more do you want?

THOMAS: Yes, I know. But I do need friends. Nobody wants to know me for who I am, so I end up going to people who will talk to me, who will understand and listen to me for once. I am so tired of being persistently judged and being told I am an outcast. But, ho hum. Life goes on. Could you tell your personal assistant to mind his own business in future? One day, if I come face to face with him, I am not quite sure what I will do. I might politely disfigure him.

FREDERICK: You will do nothing of the sort, young man. Penchard has far more qualities than you will acquire in a lifetime.

THOMAS: He must be your other missing son.

FREDERICK: Get out! Get out now!

THOMAS: With great joy, Father. Have a good day, and when you see Mr Tunnell, Father, give him my regards and tell him he has terrific buns in his shop. See you later, Ben, and thanks for the lolly.

THOMAS *exits the study. He leaves the door wide open.* MR DEVEREUX *quickly shuts the door.*

FREDERICK: What an absolute nightmare! To think he has the same blood running through his veins as mine.

BENJAMIN: You should be nicer to him, Father. All he needs is a little care and attention. If you talk to him properly he does communicate very well.

FREDERICK: I shall leave that up to you. I do not have time to persevere. I have far more important things to do. Anyway, where were we?

BENJAMIN: (*Exasperated*)   I honestly cannot remember.

FREDERICK: As I was saying, who said life was fair? Benjamin, why do you think God gave all of us brains? If life were so darned simple and easy, the poor organ would feel completely useless and wasted. Then the social perception would be that we are burdened with a ball of disease for which we have no purpose. People would constantly question the need for a brain. Benjamin, you are intertwining a stupendous web of personal avarice and intolerable obstinacy. That surely takes brains, does it not? Why not utilise your brain to solve all this mess and let us all breathe easily?

BENJAMIN: My patience is quite overstretched. I will leave you for a moment's peace. Thank you for the drink, Father.

FREDERICK: Eh, please finish your drink before you leave.

BENJAMIN: I'm not so thirsty after all.

As BENJAMIN *exits,* MR DEVEREUX *finishes the last of his drink.*

SCENE THREE

AUNTIE SOPHIE *and* VERONICA *have returned from a visit to Fethambridge.* AUNTIE SOPHIE *is the only sister of* MR DEVEREUX *and lives in the family mansion. She is in her late fifties. She is a spinster. She is of medium stature, corpulent and fair. She has her hair always tied up in a bun.* VERONICA DEVEREUX *is* FREDERICK*'s second wife. She is in her forties. She appears tall, slim and of medium build. She has an honest and friendly nature.* VERONICA *and* AUNTIE SOPHIE *are chalk and cheese. As they both enter the study together, they are bickering.* FREDERICK *is seated behind his desk, facing the window. On hearing* SOPHIE *and* VERONICA*'s unruly arrival, he turns round.*

SOPHIE: Why are you always intent on making me feel so imperceptive in front of other people? Why can't you for once follow my lead?

VERONICA: I do not wish to support any of your conceited ideas. I don't want people to think the same about me as they do about you. I happen to have a genuine personality!

SOPHIE: Conceited? Is that your word for superior? All you had to do was agree with me. Just nod and grin. Example – if somebody asks 'does this colour suit me?' and they want you to compliment them, you reply with 'oh yes, of course it does, you look lovely'. But really, the colour is repulsive and they look awful. Can you understand that illustration? Can you grasp its essence?

VERONICA: So when we go out I am supposed to mimic a rag doll? I thought I had a life of my own?

SOPHIE: And Fred, you wouldn't have believed your ears

when she started talking about Thomas and his uncivilised habits. You should know not to speak the truth, you silly woman!
VERONICA: There is nothing wrong in stating the truth, Sophie.
FREDERICK: Ladies, could I please just for a minute have your attention?
SOPHIE: What people do not know won't hurt them. These people are easy to mislead. Family will believe any sort of explanation you give them.
VERONICA: We have used your excuse a hundred times. Don't you think that trick is quite old?
SOPHIE: And we never talk about how much there is or was in the family safe. That is private and confidential.
FREDERICK: Veronica, did you really tell them?
SOPHIE: No, Frederick, my sweet sister-in-law went further than that. When asked about young Ben's issue with this wretched girl, she almost told all. If I hadn't interrupted the frightful conversation, she would have ruined everything!
VERONICA: You know that's not true. I did not reveal so much. They seem to know half of it already. People find out this sort of information very quickly.
FREDERICK: All the more reason to cover it up and not join in. You quite simply change the subject of the conversation.
SOPHIE: And to top it all off, Luke Fitzroy was there, expressing his overwhelming gesture of goodwill towards your Veronica. You would have been so ashamed of her, Fred. She was all over him like a passionate rash.
FREDERICK: Is that true?
SOPHIE: Of course it is. Why are you asking her?
VERONICA: Have you quite finished, Sophie? Fred, we were only making polite conversation. He was telling me about his family and how he had just lost his youngest son to epilepsy.
FREDERICK: Oh, how awful.

SOPHIE: Well the way you were pouting your lips and ogling him, I thought you were pursuing one of your personal hobbies!

FREDERICK: Sophie!

SOPHIE: Blake Tarney was there as well. He said that he was looking forward to Benjamin and Michelle's wedding! Your wife was talking so encouragingly about the whole fiasco. Veronica, you were supposed to say, 'there is no Michelle in Benjamin's life. I'm sorry I have no idea what you're talking about.' And leave it at that. But oh no, you have to make things complicated.

VERONICA: I find it extremely difficult to lie.

SOPHIE: You have been in this family long enough to understand our household regulations. We cover up the damaging truth by either denying it or embellishing it with an alternative story so that our impeccable reputation is not tarnished. Especially in front of our envious and spiteful relations.

FREDERICK: Veronica, why do you keep forgetting?

SOPHIE: The words that you are looking for are utter foolhardiness. Of all the people within this mansion, I had to go with her! Fred, why couldn't I have gone on my own or better still taken Nancy or Penny?

FREDERICK: Veronica seemed like the best choice. She represents me.

SOPHIE: Veronica makes everyone within this family look like a fool. What I so effortlessly cover up she seems determined to pour hot water all over, so that the painful wound is shamefully opened.

VERONICA: I don't care how you perceive my mannerisms, Sophie, I am still considered popular and, I quote, 'a very good laugh'. Nobody sees you as the humorous or gregarious type.

SOPHIE: Fred, did you hear that? She is a good laugh. Of course you would be. Any more make-up and you would look like the ideal clown of Fethambridge!

FREDERICK: Sophie, please!
VERONICA: Jealousy makes people do all sorts of things, doesn't it, Sophie?
SOPHIE: I am not jealous. Why would I be jealous?
VERONICA: Look at what you have and look at what I have.
SOPHIE: Well, at least I presented myself with respectable formality and throughout the ceremony I was able to hold my head up high. My charisma was infallible even if I do say so myself. You, on the other hand, were too busy showing the entire crowd your imposing cleavage. That dress certainly does you no favours. I should have dropped you off at the circus downtown. I'm sure they would have found some use for another woman in a flashy dress.
VERONICA: It's called style, Sophie. Something you have very little knowledge of.
SOPHIE: Generally speaking when you have very little up here (*she points to her head*), you decide to make up for the lack of attention by spilling out your breasts. I was watching. Whilst I was enjoying the exquisite fruit, your wife was displaying melons!
FREDERICK: You're being coarse and insensitive now, ladies. Just let this go, please? Both of you. Your only commitment to each other is to be civil.
SOPHIE: I am fully aware of what the small print is, but does she know?
VERONICA: That's all very well, but, Sophie, are you conscious of my small print? Are you aware of the fact that some of us prefer to do things differently? Do you fully understand the concept of telling the truth? Or are you a spineless creature that has to crawl under cracked stones when reality is too real?
FREDERICK: Veronica, dear, one of the maids was looking for you earlier regarding some of those old gowns that you wish to throw out. I think she wants to ask for them.

VERONICA: That must be Meesha. I promised to show her the worn-out garments before I got rid of them.
FREDERICK: You'd better run along before she decides to retire to her quarters.
VERONICA: Don't be silly, Fred. I have plenty of time on my hands.
FREDERICK: Veronica, that was a subtle hint asking you to leave. To put an end to this unstinting feud.
SOPHIE: How amusing! You're not as clever as you speak.
VERONICA: One of my noticeable fortes is that I always speak my mind. One of your noticeable strengths is that you say one thing but you mean another. Again proving that you are not truthful.
SOPHIE: Do you know what else she did today? One of the nasty Braydees was there and she had the gall to say hello.
FREDERICK: Which one?
SOPHIE: Norman Braydee. Veronica immersed herself in the conversation to such an extent that I thought we would never leave!
VERONICA: It's very hard to ignore someone who is looking straight at you. All of a sudden we made eye contact, and I couldn't think of anything else to do so I greeted him politely. I was just being civil.
SOPHIE: Civil to our enemy?
FREDERICK: Ever since I testified against his brother he's been after me. Until he causes some proper damage to us he will not rest. And you said hello to him?
VERONICA: It was only a moment's gesture.
FREDERICK: Veronica? Meesha's waiting.
SOPHIE: You can try as much as you like, but always remember I have far more support than you do. So you can talk all you want.
VERONICA: (*Sarcastically*)   It is always a great pleasure to speak with you, Sophie.

She exits quickly.

FREDERICK: So how was the demeaning wedding?
SOPHIE: You didn't tell me Marja had given birth to twins!
FREDERICK: You've never really been one to show delight on hearing good news. Especially to new arrivals.
SOPHIE: But she already has children. In fact, three of them. Another two surely makes her disgusting? I mean, in this day and age five children would cause more trouble than they are worth.
FREDERICK: That's an awful thing to say, Sophie.
SOPHIE: Precisely. That is the truth behind having too many children. It's absolutely sickening.
FREDERICK: So did anything else happen?
SOPHIE: Had you shown up, you probably would have enjoyed yourself and Veronica would not have caused so much grief.
FREDERICK: I do not like attending little people's weddings,
SOPHIE: But he's your nephew, Frederick! If you recall, you promised Stuart's father you would take care of them when he passed away.
FREDERICK: I did nothing of the sort. That was a complete misunderstanding. I was there by my brother's side, as one would be, and he said many things. I did not respond to any of his requests. The kind of life that he decided to lead was entirely his doing, until all of a sudden due to his negligent manner he falls ill and on his deathbed starts to assume that I will automatically take care of his family. That's just not possible. I can't just drop everything and take full responsibility for a family of four! Neither do I have the patience or the financial capacity, at least willingly.
SOPHIE: His mother seemed rather upset when I said that you were busy with other matters and would see them at a later date.
FREDERICK: My stupid and naive nephew decided to marry a thief. Surely you don't expect me to honour her presence within the Devereux hierarchy? I mean, the contemptible bride was caught red-handed as you know very well. Standing in the same room would have been mortifying.

SOPHIE: That was four years ago, Fred. Nobody remembers that anymore.
FREDERICK: I obviously do!
SOPHIE: Then suddenly my heart came to a stagnant halt. The inglorious Roy Minster attended as well.
FREDERICK: Oh, you poor thing! Does he still want to marry you?
SOPHIE: He was trying so hard to impress me with his timorous charm and preposterous talk. He looked into my eyes and attempted to draw nearer and nearer until I could smell his tainted cologne. If I hadn't moved he would have been rubbing himself against my body. I thought I was going to vomit all over the floor.
FREDERICK: Well, he does have a lot of money, Sophie. He may be worth a chance.
SOPHIE: Frederick, he has halitosis. He was seconds way from melting my face. Do you realise now that I will have to scour my eyebrows and forehead and meticulously shampoo my hair?
FREDERICK: But he has the right combination for mental stability and freedom of thought. He has real money.
SOPHIE: I suppose that reeks as well. Fred, I have no intention of looking for a beau, especially at my age. They can all try as much as they like, but I am not interested. I have already spent half of my life in solitude. I do not want to rock the boat.
FREDERICK: The man seems relentless.
SOPHIE: Frederick, I do not wish to talk about it any further.
FREDERICK: I told him to go. I thought that if he persevered he would eventually make a good impression.
SOPHIE: One minute it's Veronica and the next minute it's you. Why are you both so eager to get rid of me?
FREDERICK: It's nothing like that at all. I just want to see you happy. To have a good, successful partner within your life. We have all moved on except for you.

SOPHIE: I have moved on. Time has made me move on. I have aged gracefully. I have you and my nephews and nieces. What more could I want?

FREDERICK: You need a faithful partner who will be around all the time. You need to feel loved and you need to be able to reciprocate.

SOPHIE: I know who I love, but you always seem intent on ruining that picture.

FREDERICK: All right. I give up.

SOPHIE: And in any case, if I leave this mansion Veronica will spoil everything with her high and mighty attitude. Someone needs to be here to keep a vigilant eye on her.

FREDERICK: I wish you two would get along for once.

SOPHIE: She is a different creature from me. I have feelings that are beyond her comprehension, and her unsophisticated nature is, quite truthfully, frightening in today's society. I know I am a giving person but I cannot give too much. The buck stops here. All this anguish would not have happened if you hadn't married her.

FREDERICK: A pointless issue, Sophie! Twenty-five years have passed now! I wish you would let it go.

SOPHIE: Loni was far better. She was a woman of substance who most certainly knew her place within society. She had such grace. Why do the good and decent die so quickly and the wasted and disrespectful linger on to poison our minds and humiliate us?

FREDERICK: You need to talk to Benjamin.

SOPHIE: Again? I'm getting rather irritated with that boy.

FREDERICK: This time it may be easier, because we have had a significant turn of events.

SOPHIE: Such as?

FREDERICK: Michelle Buckley is no longer with us.

SOPHIE: What do you mean, she is no longer with us?

FREDERICK: Due to an unexpected error, Michelle has left us and started her new life beyond the heavens.

SOPHIE: Are you in any way responsible?
FREDERICK: Absolutely not! But I am euphoric. Fate has played an ace.
SOPHIE: Does Benjamin know?
FREDERICK: No. I need you to break the unfavourable news to him, gently, or actually, come to think of it, continue pursuing the idea that Michelle is not only bad for his health but bad for the family name and so on. Pretend that she is alive and well.
SOPHIE: I have delivered my fair share of lectures and speeches, but to no avail. Why can't Veronica do it? Surely the mother of the child should know how to deal with her son?
FREDERICK: But you have a wealth of wisdom. Ben likes talking to you. (*Pause*) Oh, my God! It's Veronica's birthday today. I completely forgot.
SOPHIE: She's too old to have a birthday. Birthdays are for children!

There is a knock at the door. Veronica enters.

VERONICA: Sorry to interrupt, but you left this in the car. Max found it. (*She holds out a navy blue shawl.*)
SOPHIE: (*remaining motionless and sombre*)   If you could put it back where it was and next time please ask before you touch my belongings. It is rather annoying when I know exactly what I am doing whilst someone else assumes I do not!
VERONICA: I was only trying to help.
FREDERICK: Veronica, dear, happy birthday.
VERONICA: Oh, you remembered!
SOPHIE: I would be delighted if you would leave us in peace to continue our important conversation ... you know, the one that you so rudely interrupted without thinking twice.
FREDERICK: We'll celebrate later.

VERONICA: I did knock on the door.

She exits silently as SOPHIE *watches her like a hawk.*

FREDERICK: You could have been nicer, it is her birthday.
SOPHIE: Why change a lifetime's habit?
FREDERICK: 'Happy birthday, Veronica.' That's all you have to say.
SOPHIE: I just don't understand why her birthday is such an issue. It's not that important. After all, we are all going to die some day. It's just a show. 'Oh, look at me, I was born and now I'm going to make a big deal about it.' Then everyone around you has the burden of having to show care.
FREDERICK: You are very bitter today!
SOPHIE: Frederick, history has made me bitter, surely you should know that.

There is another knock on the door. VERONICA *re-enters.*

VERONICA: Sorry to break the law again by interrupting your private conversation, but Lawrence is here with the marquees, Fred.
SOPHIE: Frederick has instructed me to say 'happy birthday' to you, so there, I have said it. I don't particularly see the point, but whatever! What a dismal excuse to draw on to waste an entire day!
FREDERICK: Sophie!
SOPHIE: Oh, was I not supposed to say that?
FREDERICK: Could you kindly inform Lawrence I am on my way, dear.
VERONICA: I shall do that. See you later.

VERONICA *smiles as she exits. She completely ignores* SOPHIE.

SOPHIE: Any news on the burglar?
FREDERICK: No, not really.
SOPHIE: How much did you say the final amount was?
FREDERICK: Just over £7,000.
SOPHIE: Wasn't there more money in the safe than £7,000?
FREDERICK: There was £19,000 in total.
SOPHIE: So why didn't the scoundrel take all the money? What really annoys me is that this vagabond is sitting around somewhere, counting our money and laughing about it. Insulting us viciously and criticising us with his or her harmful tongue.
FREDERICK: The scoundrel that you are talking about is someone we know.
SOPHIE: Who? Who is it?
FREDERICK: Well, at first I thought the mansion's staff had something to do with it, but then after the incident I traced everyone's movements on that day and I came to the conclusion that no member of staff could have done it.
SOPHIE: What about an outsider who may have been given the information in advance and who then crept into the mansion whilst everyone else was busy?
FREDERICK: An outsider could be a possibility, but unfortunately it isn't.
SOPHIE: Tell me, then, who is it?
FREDERICK: I'm afraid to say it's Thomas.
SOPHIE: Thomas who?
FREDERICK: My deplorable son.
SOPHIE: Why? Why would he do that?
FREDERICK: Because he is a diseased boy. He only thinks about his own needs. He lives in a world of his own and is constantly in need of money to satisfy his dreadful habit. He asks for money and then he steals money.
SOPHIE: Are you going to confront him?
FREDERICK: There is no point. He always admits to whatever I want to accuse him of. He finds it very amusing.

Subsequently, he will promise to pay back every penny and that is all. He only speaks with enthusiasm, he does not believe in activating his pledges.

SOPHIE: I thought only you and I knew the combination?

FREDERICK: He must have studied very hard to acquire the number sequence.

SOPHIE: What if by any chance you are wrong?

FREDERICK: I wish I was.

SOPHIE: Shall I have a chat to him?

FREDERICK: No, not now. As long as I know where he is, the lecture can wait. Instead you talk to Benjamin. I had a little discussion with him earlier. He was very uncooperative.

SOPHIE: Have you ever thought what would happen if Benjamin chose to leave home?

FREDERICK: No, he wouldn't do that. He who lives in luxury can never run away and stay with the little folk with meagre amenities. His expectations are too high, and once he goes down a few classes he will realise that the difference is titanic. He will feel himself drowning. I know there is someone out there for him. We just have to keep looking, that's all. Maybe the person we are looking for is closer than we think.

SOPHIE: Frederick why do I sense that you are up to something?

FREDERICK: It was Nancy's idea. Quite a brilliant one indeed. Let's say the annual Devereux extravaganza this year will prove to be very meaningful for not only the usual business reasons but also for our social welfare. He is the sole heir to this domain. I cannot have him make a total fool of himself or us, so that is why his sister has come up with this very pleasing proposal.

SOPHIE: Well, what about Thomas? Where does he come into all this? By being the elder brother, surely he is to be the sole inheritor of your domain?

FREDERICK: Sophie, he is nothing. He is absolutely useless

and a thief. I wish he would die and leave us all alone. I cannot understand why a son of mine would turn out like this. I have tried so hard to make him into the kind of man that any father would be proud of, but sadly he has chosen a path of indignity and fallen into a deep pit of depression. No one can rescue him. The only person he confides in is Loni.

SOPHIE: I know he has done many horrendous things in the past, but he is your son. He is a part of you. After all, you do love him, don't you?

FREDERICK: There is absolutely no point in loving a no-hoper. All he does is drink. He has no sense of direction. He has no plans for his future and above all he does not care what he is doing to this family. I should have destroyed him when he was a baby. Thomas's depression only proves how selfish he really is. When you are constantly miserable, the only thing you succeed in is believing that society owes you a great debt for the mental injustice you are suffering. He prefers to trap himself, so that neither you nor I can help heal any of his insecurities. Even if I gave him the entire world, he would turn round and say, 'why are you making me more miserable than I already am?'

SOPHIE: If only Loni was here!

FREDERICK: Maybe if she were alive today she would have been able to sort things out. She would have beaten some sense into him.

SOPHIE: If only Loni knew, then she would see what an incompetent father you actually are. Why are you always trying to put the onus on someone else when you can easily put it right? Loni died twenty-six years ago. A long long time ago. I'm sure she is looking down at you thinking 'Oh, for goodness sake, Frederick, why have you not got the hang of things yet?'

FREDERICK: I would love to chat further but I must dash. Lawrence is waiting.

SOPHIE: You didn't even offer me a drink!

FREDERICK: Well, the drinks are over there. Help yourself!
SOPHIE: No, thank you. I'm not thirsty anyway. I suppose I'd better fetch my shawl from the car!

FREDERICK *picks up a few papers from his desk and exits.*
SOPHIE *follows.*

SCENE FOUR

NANCY *and* PENELOPE DEVEREUX *are relaxing in* PENELOPE*'s huge ornate bedroom.* PENELOPE *is a full-time teacher of English Literature and* NANCY *helps out part time.* NANCY *also owns a specialist jewellery shop in Fezaria-Aston.* NANCY *is 31 years old, the older of the two sisters. She is tall, dark and slim. She always adopts a plain appearance and stringent manner.* PENELOPE*, 30 years old, is slim, dark, elegant and of medium height. She is debonair and easy-going.*

PENELOPE: . . . he goes on to say, he misses my charming smile, my infectious laughter . . .
NANCY: Oh please, you still have that terrible letter? I told you to throw that damned letter away. Daniel Sullivan has no humanitarian qualities. He was born a liar and he still is one. And besides, why do you want to meet the despicable man who brazenly walked out on you?
PENELOPE: That was two years ago. He was all mixed up back then.
NANCY: Your marriage was at stake. Your respect and self-confidence were shattered, and he brought great shame on the family. A simple apology on a pathetic piece of paper does not heal the sore wounds of the past. Even if he were to beg you to come back, I would quite plainly spit in his face.
PENELOPE: But this lovely letter makes him seem so different. It's as if he's really changed since he's returned from America.
NANCY: Oh, the land of the melodramatic chain of hopeless actors. Mark my words, he's up to something.

PENELOPE: Well, what if he isn't? What if this is genuine? Daniel always had an exciting dream. He wanted to be successful. He wanted the best out of his life. So what if he decided to pursue that dream? Now he's back and he sincerely wants to see me.
NANCY: He wanted success so much that he stole from us and abandoned his marriage and then fled the country.
PENELOPE: He always did say he was never worthy of me.
NANCY: He still isn't. As far as I'm concerned he has returned for the worst. Penny, he's going to turn your life upside down again. The poisonous letter is echoing so much love, sympathy and regret only to lure you into his venomous trap. Just like before. Penny, because you're blinded by his poetic words of love, you are not even listening to me.
PENELOPE: Look, Nancy, there must be a very good reason for him writing this letter. It's not just a short meaningless note. It's five whole pages of so much that he wished he hadn't done and so much remorse. Why don't you see for yourself? (*She tries to hand over the note.*)
NANCY: No, thank you. It's your private letter. Nothing to do with me. Wait till Father finds out. He's going to go mad. He hates Daniel. He hates the sight of him.
PENELOPE: I will have to talk to him. It's important that Father knows Daniel is not the kind of man he was.
NANCY: Fine! Go ahead! Make your life miserable all over again. Daniel is definitely up to his old tricks again. Now that I think about it, I can almost sense it. I bet he's lost everything in America and now he has returned penniless.
PENELOPE: I'm going to see him. I want to meet him.
NANCY: Are you going to talk to him about his other marriage to Mishty Shakar, the truly deafening and diabolical lead singer of the melodious hyenas?
PENELOPE: No, I don't think it's valid.
NANCY: Why?
PENELOPE: This is about us. I just want to concentrate on our

relationship, salvage our marriage and look forward, hopefully, to new prospects.
NANCY: Even if he's still married to Mishty, you don't care?
PENELOPE: No, not really!
NANCY: So, in your book, bigamy has a high score?
PENELOPE: I don't approve, naturally, but that doesn't mean I have to talk about it. He did what he wanted to do and now he has come to his senses. He realises his mistakes. He realises that his life is totally empty without me.
NANCY: Is that what he's put in his letter? He should have put, 'as Mishty has no money due to her failure as a screeching singer, I have decided to seek your loving assistance. So please spare me some cash. This way I can use you again and leave you to pick up the pieces and thrust you into Dr Mesner's clinic once more.'
PENELOPE: I only had two sessions with him.
NANCY: Why should you need to have any sessions with him? Penny, do you understand what actually happened to you when you let this Daniel Sullivan into your life? He played with your emotions, trapped you into thinking that as his wife you are to serve him day and night and carry out his futile commands and not question him once. Did you ever ask him, 'am I at all important to you?' Just because he couldn't afford a cook or a maid or find a decent job, he cunningly decided to marry you. And you, being naïve and stupid, did everything that he wanted. Not once did he consider your feelings. That's why he left you. If you ask me, Mishty is a perfect match for him.
PENELOPE: Well, what about second chances? If a person has done wrong and he admits to it then surely he deserves a second chance? After all, it does take a lot of courage to confess that you have made grave mistakes.
NANCY: Not if there is something lucrative at the end of it. And that's you. Penny, he is a typical example of a man who commits only to the moment. He will look into your eyes so

deeply as he will declare his undying love for you. He will perform such a benevolent and convincing act that you will not doubt him for one single second. He will talk so lovingly, so gently and so sincerely that you will want to trust him all over again.

PENELOPE: He wants to meet me at the Cerissia Hotel.

NANCY: He obviously remembers your favourite hotel. How nice of him to set a lovely, hospitable scene.

PENELOPE: You promise you won't tell anyone about the note?

NANCY: Do I have a choice?

PENELOPE: No, but I would be so grateful if you showed me some support. If Mum were alive today she would understand my feelings.

NANCY: She'd probably say the same things as me!

PENELOPE: I do hope you are wrong about him.

NANCY: I hope for your sake I am very wrong. You have finally put your career back on track and managed to get on with your life. I'd hate to see that wasted all over again.

PENELOPE: He wants to meet me this coming Tuesday. Could you cover my English Literature class for me?

NANCY: All right! Only this once. Another rendezvous on a school night and I'll have to give you detention and a hundred lines.

PENELOPE: (*she hugs* NANCY.) Oh, you're an angel! Now, what should I wear?

NANCY: Nothing too elegant. Nothing that makes you look desirable.

PENELOPE: I just want to look nice for my husband.

NANCY: May I say how well you have already fallen for his web of lies and devilish charm.

PENELOPE: Nancy, they're called feelings.

NANCY: Well, suppress them as best you can when you meet him and make sure he does all the talking, not you. See what he actually wants. If it sounds as if he is going to use you again, then I'm certain he'll eventually slip up somewhere.

PENELOPE: My instincts say that things are going to be much better now. He's going to be a changed man. I know it.
NANCY: Ink on paper always shows a different picture to reality.
PENELOPE: At least to me his intentions seem clear.
NANCY: Please don't fall for his good looks!
PENELOPE: Nancy, you're very welcome to accompany me to the Cerissia and watch.
NANCY: I think I have heard enough. Good luck for Tuesday!
PENELOPE: Daniel's always liked sky blue. I think I'll wear my sky-blue dress with the nice frilly bits.
NANCY: I hope Penchard's beady eyes don't see you meeting him. He always makes a mountain out of a molehill.
PENELOPE: Even if he does, once I am in front of Father I shall confess all and request a second chance for Daniel.
NANCY: Your kind request will be met with great antipathy. Instead Father will hunt him down like a fox in the wild and you shall cry once more.
PENELOPE: I have to take that chance. If Father does decide to disappoint me then I will have to do everything I can to protect him. It would be my responsibility.
NANCY: Fine. (*Pause*) Are you looking forward to the Dex?
PENELOPE: No. Not really. Another year, another mind-numbing Devereux extravaganza, more opulent and arrogant guests, sophisticated attire, expensive shiny jewellery, too much make-up, hundreds of glasses of drinks, excessive consumption of food, smelly and yucky caviar, boring spicy salmon bites...
NANCY: Hey, I love the salmon bites. I could eat a whole tray of them.
PENELOPE: And what about the corporate speeches? Remember last year how Mr Hugo Breldershower wouldn't finish? I was so embarrassed for him. He couldn't stop talking about his marvellous yachts and then the worst part came. His very fashionable women's lingerie talk. I didn't know where to look.

NANCY: Oh, I remember him. His faithful assistant brought in some very sexy but quite tacky samples for the rest of the guests to look at. Some were very offensive. But to Coral they were an immediate attraction, so she decided to take the black lacy bras without asking. On seeing what Coral was up to, his short fat assistant rushed over to rescue the detestable goods from her astute hands, but the moment she winked at him and stuck her tongue out and licked her lips he was putty in her hands.

PENELOPE: And then she dropped the large tray of champagne glasses, Father nearly had a heart attack and Thomas was attempting to soak up the champagne with a large sponge and wring it out in an oblong dish!

NANCY: Now, that was really embarrassing. Father locked him out of the mansion for three weeks and he had to stay with Rose and her family.

PENELOPE: You mean cousin Rose who lives in Blegly?

NANCY: No, it was Cook's house. He did say, though, that he slept on a proper bed with a small nightstand beside it.

PENELOPE: Oh! I never knew that. (*Pause*) Do you think I should invite Daniel to the Dex?

NANCY: That is an absolutely awful idea. No. You must not.

PENELOPE: Why not? Father will be too busy with his hundreds of rich guests. He won't have time to question everyone. And besides, I will make sure that when Father is at one end of the hall he is at the other end.

NANCY: What is your back-up plan in case he does spot him?

PENELOPE: Well, I'm thinking it's going to be a very hectic and demanding day so he won't make a scene until later on. By then I am certain I will have the perfect explanation!

NANCY: I love the fact that you are such a sweet and naïve dreamer. It's such a pity when people like you don't learn.

PENELOPE: I can't just sit and do nothing. I have to do something. Otherwise I'll regret it.

NANCY: Better you than me! Did the post arrive this morning?

PENELOPE: I think so. I'm sure I saw Penchard sorting it out earlier on.
NANCY: I'm expecting a very important correspondence from Louis. He's agreed to show me his valuable collection of emeralds and diamonds.
PENELOPE: Is he bonafide, Nancy?
NANCY: Who cares! I want the jewels. I don't care if he's ugly, has bad breath and has never shaved one day in his life, I just want those precious stones.
PENELOPE: Isn't that illegal?
NANCY: I am running a reputable business. My company holds some of the finest precious stones ever seen. People are full of admiration and enchanting compliments when they come to my shop. I do not have time to study criminal law or criminal psychology. I simply need the goods. If it's from crooked Cyril or dishonest Derek, I am not at all concerned. Now, if you'll excuse me I have other matters to take care of. Is Patrick here today?
PENELOPE: Who's Patrick?
NANCY: You don't know who Patrick is? He's our handsome and unbelievably scrumptious gardener, with the most beautiful torso I have ever seen.
PENELOPE: Oh, you mean Pat? He's busy on the west-wing lawn.
NANCY: Brilliant. Is this outfit too conservative?
PENELOPE: No. Not really.
NANCY: That means it is! I'll have to change into something that will make him think and see more than he should. See you at dinner.
PENELOPE: Ah, leave the poor boy alone, he's only nineteen!
NANCY: I'm just exploring my feminine instincts. That's all!
PENELOPE: You are funny, Nancy!

NANCY *exits the room hurriedly.* PENELOPE *looks excitedly at her letter once more and then holds it close to her.*

SCENE FIVE

The mansion's staff is gathered in the grand kitchen. ROSE *is in her fifties, buxom and of short height. She is the cook.* PETER, *in his twenties, very attractive, dark and tall, is one of the butlers, and* MEESHA, *one of two secondary maids, is slim, fair and of medium height.* ROSE *is busy making a large sponge cake and* MEESHA *is grouping lots of fresh vegetables on a massive wooden table.* PETER *looks on, standing behind* MEESHA.

MEESHA: Rose, please could you tell Peter to stop caressing my arse! I am getting rather infuriated, to say the least!
ROSE: Peter, please, this is a kitchen. There is no room for your dirty tricks.
PETER: (*He stops his caressing.*) Rose, I know this is a kitchen. And I also know that this is Meesha and she has a very gentle and hospitable bottom. (*He resumes the caressing.*)
MEESHA: Peter, I don't like you anymore. Well, not in that way. So will you for once keep your hands to yourself!
PETER: Why ever not? I find you absolutely gorgeous. You're one of the best I've ever had.
MEESHA: Oh, piss off! Go and shag someone else, you pervert!
ROSE: Meesha, language!
PETER: Would it help if I stopped sleeping with Jona? My time with her seems to collide with your shifts, my little sweet.
MEESHA: After having dumped you, what makes you think I would want to be with you again? You can do whatever you like. I'm not interested.
ROSE: Leave the poor girl alone, Peter.
MEESHA: If I have to I'll report you!

PETER: If you report me then I'll report you for sexual harassment within the workplace.
MEESHA: Well, what the hell are you doing now? Isn't this proper sexual harassment?
PETER: Of course it isn't! Because I have feelings attached, there is no harassment involved. You just disagree with the fact that I am touching your bottom. Would it help you if I rubbed your sexy thigh, you know, to understand how I feel about you, o adorable Meesha?
MEESHA: No it bloody well wouldn't! Just because I went out with you doesn't mean you can just come along and put your shitty hands on me! Do you have no respect for me? Do you have no shame?
PETER: All right! All right! I will stop only on one condition! You have to sleep with me one more time. That is my last wish.
ROSE: Peter, please be quiet! I do not want to hear any more of this conversation. You are very much out of line here. Apologise to Meesha and let her finish her work.
PETER: Sorry, Meesha. It's just that I love you so much and I miss you every day. Ever since you dumped me I am finding it difficult to touch anyone else's bottom. Jona has too much hair on her bottom.
ROSE: Wait a minute! Is this the Jona who lives with three other lads and claims they're all her brothers?
PETER: Yes. She has three younger brothers.
ROSE: And they all seem to have Adam's apples!
PETE: Yeah, so?
ROSE: Don't you see?
MEESHA: Oh my God, Peter, your girlfriend is a man!
PETER: No she's not. She is a woman. All woman!
MEESHA: You idiot, you haven't done anything with her, have you? The other night, when you had your first date with her, it did end pretty quickly! Coral caught you climbing through her bedroom window. She said she saw Jona running after you in the street.

PETER: I just forgot where the door was, all right? Besides, I was looking for a short cut.
ROSE: Is there something you're hiding, Peter?
PETER: Look, you girls don't understand. I am particularly sensitive about these issues. And besides, it's private.
MEESHA: Where did you meet him?
PETER: It's her, all right?
MEESHA: (*begins to laugh*) With an Adam's apple? It's rather huge, don't you think? I've seen Jona and she is not very feminine.
PETER: All right, all right! My first date was an absolute disaster. Jona was trying to show me something, I then got a little scared and I screamed. And then I thought I should run out before things got out of hand. So I rushed out to get some fresh air. It was all very overwhelming!
ROSE: Did you have no idea that Jona had always been a man dressed as a woman?
MEESHA: You went out with a man! You dumb old twit! Serves you right for going out with a different woman every day! I bet that when you caressed his bottom he was as excited as a panda.
PETER: That was a complete mistake, all right? I was hoping for something exciting. Unfortunately, that excitement was very terrifying and short-lived.
MEESHA: So when are we going to meet her or him?
PETER: That's not funny!
ROSE: (*laughing*) Of course it's funny. You had no idea that Jona was all man.
PETER: Laugh all you want, but now I have a date with Tracey on Friday, Melanie on Saturday and Hayley on Sunday.
MEESHA: Why are you looking at me like that? I'm not jealous. They're all stupid and ugly, and Hayley is violent, especially if you don't let her do what she wants.
PETER: No she's not. One of your scare tactics? This time it isn't going to work.

MEESHA: Last guy she went out with was really fussy and a bit bossy, so she went to the voodoo joint in Jazar Corner and turned his thingy purple. He hasn't been out on a date since.
PETER: I don't believe in that voodoo rubbish!
MEESHA: Well, when she turns your thingy purple, you will believe it!
PETER: Maybe I should cancel with Hayley?
MEESHA: Pass me the cauliflowers, Peter?
ROSE: Peter, love, when are you going to settle down and have a proper life? You know, a good wife and a loving family?
PETER: (*passing the cauliflowers*) When I get bored of playing the field, Rose. I can't settle down knowing that I have so much potential in that department!
MEESHA: Hardly! I can certainly vouch for that.
PETER: Hey, that's not true! You said yourself that I am amazing!
ROSE: Could we possibly talk about something else?
PETER: Women find me irresistible. Rose, wouldn't you go out with me?
ROSE: If you were well behaved, yes, of course I would.
PETER: I am the most eligible attractive bachelor there is. I am a totally lip-smacking kind of guy.
MEESHA: Oh please! If it weren't for me nobody would know who you were. I put you on the Fezaria-Aston map.
PETER: Oh, so what. I'm still attractive.
MEESHA: Is that what you chant in front of the mirror every day to give your ego a little boost, even though you are not?
PETER: You know I take that sort of thing seriously.
MEESHA: That is really interesting, because monkeys are attractive too. And the other night I met the most eligible gibbon there ever was!
ROSE: Either of you tell me what the time is?
PETER: Time for Meesha to shut up, I think!
MEESHA: It's four-thirty, Rose.

ROSE: Right. The sponge cake is going in now. Please keep an eye.

PETER: I don't understand what your problem is. You went out with me, remember?

MEESHA: That was just a stupid bet with Coral. Nothing to do with you.

PETER: Pardon?

MEESHA: Oh shit!

PETER: You were saying?

MEESHA: It was just one of those things. Coral bet that I wouldn't be able to get you interested in me because I was not seen as your type. So to prove her wrong, I went after you and it happened. I won ten pounds and she bought me dinner! The money came in handy for some really nice earrings.

PETER: Coral, that bloody bitch!

ROSE: Peter!

PETER: You are a bitch too, Meesha! You used me!

MEESHA: Oh get over it! The next day you went out with Patsy Norton!

PETER: Oh yes, I did, didn't I?

CORAL, *in her late twenties, is the principal maid. She is slim, tall and has short dark hair. She is always expressive with her speech. She enters the kitchen hurriedly and immediately hails everyone's attention.*

CORAL: You have got to look out of the window. Look at what's happening on the west-wing lawn.

They all rush and stare out of the window. PETER *plants himself right behind* MEESHA *and begins to caress her bottom again.*

MEESHA: Peter, will you take your bloody hands off of my arse?

PETER: No! I like it! Plus you smell nice.
CORAL: Will you two just shut your traps and look? Nancy is trying to get it on with Pat!
ROSE: Well I never!
CORAL: Talk about desperate times!
ROSE: He must be half her age!
PETER: What is she doing with her chest?
MEESHA: It looks as if she's aiming it towards his face.
PETER: But she hasn't got anything there! It's flat!
ROSE: Must you look so closely?
PETER: What the hell is she doing with her leg?
CORAL: She's rubbing it against his thigh, I think.
MEESHA: Do you think she's had a few glasses?
ROSE: No. When she's drunk she acts very weird. She looks perfectly sober to me.
PETER: You know, Pat's such a nice guy. I hope he doesn't leave because of her.
CORAL: Oh my God, she's touching his shoulder.
MEESHA: Now the chin.
PETER: We should record all of this on tape then ask for a pay rise. If they refuse, we show the tape!
CORAL: The leg has come down now.
MEESHA: I just hope Pat doesn't freak out.
ROSE: I thought she had some form of dignity.
PETER: She's not very good at winking, is she?
ROSE: Hey, Peter, looks like she's stolen your moves. She's now caressing Pat's bottom too!
CORAL: I didn't think she was that miserable!
ROSE: Well, she has passed her sell-by date. I saw her removing some grey hair the other day from her jacket.
MEESHA: Oh, now she's going for the big one! She's awfully close to it.
PETER: What's 'the big one'?
CORAL: For a smart guy you are really dumb.
PETER: I have no idea what you're talking about.

MEESHA: Shit! Shit! Shit! She's going for his...

All of a sudden PENCHARD's *footsteps come thundering down into the kitchen. He is in his forties. He is of medium height, not so thin, and has fair wavy hair. He wears thick-rimmed glasses. Like* MR DEVEREUX, *he adopts an air of superiority. On entering the room he finds all four members of staff busy gaping out of the window.*

PENCHARD: I had no idea that your various responsibilities allowed you to waste time looking out of the window!

All four are a little shaken by PENCHARD's *sudden entrance. Immediately, with great speed, they scuttle back to their work.*

PENCHARD: Is anyone going to tell me what's so fascinating? (*He is about to have a look.*)
CORAL: (*getting in his way*) Oh, Penchard, I have been meaning to talk to you about something. Em ... em ... are we getting a pay rise this year?
PENCHARD: Coral, with the kind of service you provide, do you honestly think a pay rise would be justified?
CORAL: By the way, that colour really suits you and the shoes are quite remarkable.
PENCHARD: Why, thank you!
PETER: Actually the tie really doesn't go with anything. It's too bright. I remember seeing that type of tie around a dead man's neck down Nectar Grove. He looked really pale. Two weeks later the cockroaches had a great feast. And your shoes must be ex-clown footwear!
CORAL: Oh, Penchard, don't listen to Peter. He's just jealous. Aren't you, Peter? (*She widens her eyes and gestures at Peter so that he agrees.*)
PETER: (*sarcastically*) Yes, I am frequently jealous of you because of your eye-catching and phenomenal dress sense. I wish I could turn heads like you, pretty Penchard!

PENCHARD: I am sure you are. Now, I have come here for an important reason. As you may already understand, I am not the type of person who simply swans into the mansion's kitchen and talks to ordinary staff, but today I come to you with a dilemma.
MEESHA: Oh how common of you!
ROSE: We are utterly privileged by your presence. The atmosphere was so drab until you came along!
PENCHARD: Has anyone seen today's post? I left it on the mailing desk and I only disappeared for a few seconds, then on my return it had all been taken. Do any of you have any idea where it could be?
ROSE: Sponge cake!
PENCHARD: What?
ROSE: I need to check the oven.
PETER: Wait a minute, are you accusing us of stealing the post? When you know very well that nobody in this mansion would dare do such a thing. After all, this is the Devereux mansion. No one bound by the rigid rules of this household would even think twice of such a thing! You mean-spirited, pompous git.
PENCHARD: I beg your pardon!
MEESHA: Maybe we have taken it?
CORAL: Meesha, please, stop fooling around. (*with gritted teeth*) We don't have the post.
MEESHA: I was only winding him up, Coral. Penchard, you are such a gormless sweetheart, no one here has taken the post. I'm afraid you're in the shit yourself. Now, the way out is that way. (*She indicates the door.*)
PENCHARD: There is certainly no need for this sort of behaviour or foul-mouthed language. Unfortunate people like you have no concept of etiquette. You're all very lucky I'm in a good mood today. I am not going to report any of you, but next time I will not yield. I have got my eye on all of you. One false move and you'll be wondering where your next meal is coming from. You have been warned!

ROSE: Good day to you, Penchard!

PENCHARD *exits briskly with his hands behind his back.*

PETER: What an absolutely stupid arrogant pretentious ugly git! If I had a wish I would tie him up in a sack and then beat the hell out of him with a massive steel pole. Who the hell does he think he is?

CORAL: Phew! That was close. When Penchard disappeared for a little bit I grabbed the post from his desk and ran back here. (*She puts her hand inside her uniform, draws out quite a few envelopes and puts them all on the floor.*) I just wanted to know if Mr Devereux definitely has a mistress. There must be a note somewhere here. I overheard one of the other maids talking about it yesterday. Apparently she's very beautiful and kind and there may be plans to bring her into the mansion.

ROSE: What about Veronica?

CORAL: I'm not sure what's going to happen to her. Perhaps she'll be made to leave.

PETER: Or they might want to butcher her!

ROSE: A mistress, eh? I knew it. He treats Veronica with such insolence.

MEESHA: Why do all the nice ones have to leave?

PETER: What about Auntie Sumo, I mean Auntie Sophie? Is she still looking for her husband?

MEESHA: I thought it was her son. Didn't her husband die many years ago?

ROSE: But she's never married.

PETER: Oooohh! I get it. She obviously slept with someone and had his baby. Raised by someone else and now she wants to get to know him. That could be it.

ROSE: My only knowledge on the matter is that she does have a son somewhere but they are not allowed to talk about it. Her father made absolutely sure about that.

PETER: Sounds like another bully!
CORAL: Oh, this one is from the debt collectors.
PETER: Open it! Open it!
MEESHA: I'll put the kettle on.
ROSE: I've warned all three of you about this sort of thing. If you get caught, you will be very sorry. Mr Devereux will kill you.
PETER: We're not scared of the bully.
MEESHA: That peach-coloured envelope over there, isn't that the kind of envelope Madame Lubelle uses for her clients?
ROSE: Look, everyone, Pat is running away from Nancy! Run faster, my boy, faster, faster!

They all peer out of the window again.

CORAL: Hard luck, Nancy! He's too fast for you, silly tart!
MEESHA: Open the door for him, I think he's running this way. Open it! Open it!

CORAL *opens the back door wide for the gardener. With loud breathlessness and profuse perspiration* PATRICK *rushes in, leaving* NANCY *far behind. On* PATRICK*'s entry* CORAL *very quickly shuts the door.* PATRICK *wipes his brow.*

PATRICK: Thank you. Thank you so much.
MEESHA: I bet the job description didn't tell you about her then?
PATRICK: No. Thank goodness I didn't run into a dead end. She would have been all over me.
PETER: Here, take a seat! You seem very breathless!
PATRICK: She's really full of herself and quite smutty. She couldn't stop touching me! I was so scared!
ROSE: You poor thing!
CORAL: Well, who could blame her? You are rather gorgeous! So do you really like gardening? I've got a lovely garden if you have time!

ROSE: Coral!
PATRICK: It's not that fun, actually. It's quite boring! Landscaping isn't quite my trade.
MEESHA: So why do it?
PATRICK: I'm here to find out some important information.
PETER: What kind of information?
CORAL: Are you from a secret spy company? Oh I get it! You're undercover!
PATRICK: Well, to cut a long story short, I'm looking for my sister Michelle.
MEESHA: Michelle who?
PATRICK: Michelle Buckley, she went missing a week ago. We've been looking everywhere for her. Unfortunately, the authorities are hopeless. They just don't want to know.
PETER: Surely someone can help?
PATRICK: If you put good money on the table then they will listen to you. Otherwise it's a waste of time for them. If I were rich I'm sure we would have found out where Michelle was by now. My parents are very distressed at the moment. We simply cannot make head nor tail of this. She's never been one to just disappear
CORAL: Wait a minute, wait a minute. Michelle Buckley is your sister? Michelle Buckley is Benjamin's girlfriend, isn't she?
PATRICK: Yes. She is. She seems to enjoy being with him. My father has spoken to her on numerous occasions, asking her to end her relationship, but she's remained stubborn. She loves Benjamin Devereux dearly and she is very happy. She doesn't care about the consequences.
PETER: Wait till Frederick Devereux gets involved. I'm surprised that he hasn't done something about it already.
MEESHA: I reckon he's up to something. It seems awfully quiet at the moment. I haven't heard any of them talking about it.
PATRICK: Has Benjamin been around the mansion lately?

ROSE: I haven't seen him for a while.
MEESHA: I think I saw him yesterday. I went to clean his room and it was a bit of a mess. Normally he's rather tidy. It looked as if he was packing.
CORAL: Are you thinking what I'm thinking? Do you think they're planning to elope?
PATRICK: You could be right. I was talking to my parents earlier today and they believe the same too. I have got to find out where she is. I need to find her before Frederick Devereux unleashes his wild dogs on her.
ROSE: Why can't they just let it be? They obviously love each other and want to be together.
PETER: The kettle's boiled. I said the kettle's boiled, you tart!
MEESHA: All right! All right! Which letter are we opening?
ROSE: Open that blue one.
PETER: Get me a bowl, Meesha. We're going for the blue one first.
CORAL: (*She hands over the blue letter from the pile of mail.*) Why blue?
ROSE: It looks as if it's from the police.
PETER: (*He takes the letter and then the bowl.*) Right. Let's see what it says.
PATRICK: You know you're not supposed to open other people's letters. Letters are private and confidential if not addressed to you.
CORAL, MEESHA and PETER: Oh shut up, Pat!
ROSE: Now, now, children!
PETER: (*He unseals the letter successfully.*)   Ready? 'Thank you for your advance. The body has been disposed of very carefully. There are no traces of any evidence. Paperwork indicates female committed suicide. Any other form of official procedure will be amended immediately. You need not be concerned in any capacity. If we can be of any further assistance, please do not hesitate to contact us. D.S.P.' Well I never!

PATRICK: He said female. Do you think it means Michelle?
PETER: Good job we opened that letter. You and your 'private and confidential'. See what's going on behind our backs? Cold-blooded murder and bribery within legal quarters. He's got them all in his pocket. That means none of us will ever be safe in this town.
CORAL: Well, we don't know for sure that it's Michelle, do we?
ROSE: Patrick, love, it can't be. You have to understand that Mr Devereux is a professional when it comes to dealing with the underworld. I've been here long enough to know and, believe me, I am fully aware of what goes on. This doesn't seem right. All that effort for one particular case. Normally, the matter is far more complex.
PETER: Yes, we all know what kind of man Mr Devereux is, but the real question is who is this girl?
MEESHA: Poor girl. Whoever she is, she must have suffered so much pain.
PATRICK: It's got to be Michelle.
Coral: Look, we do not know for certain if it's her. One thing for sure is that Mr Frederick Devereux owns the police.
PETER: I wonder when this all happened?
PATRICK: It has to be Michelle.
CORAL: I wish that letter said more so that we could really find out who that dead girl was.
PETER: I wonder how many people he has actually killed.
ROSE: Don't go down that road, Peter. There are certain details that will leave you gasping for air!
PATRICK: I guess my work has been done. It's her. Michelle's body has been disposed of. I have to leave. I have to go home and tell my parents.
PETER: Just wait a second. You can't leave. You have to stay and get to the bottom of this. You need to find out the real truth yourself. The letter is your prime lead but now you have to find sufficient proof.

PATRICK: If only she had listened to Father. He warned her countless times not to enter into this dangerous relationship. Why didn't she listen? Now she's dead. Why did this have to happen to her?

CORAL: I think I'll go and put the post back on Penchard's desk. We've found out enough for one day.

PATRICK: I swear Mr Devereux is going to pay such a heavy price. I'm not going to just stand and turn the other way. So what if he's rich and corrupted, I want him to realise his mistake.

ROSE: Patrick, love, please calm down. We need the facts first. Even if it is him, you must understand there is no way you can overpower this tyrant. If you try to threaten him in any way he will hunt you down, destroy your family and friends, and then he will slaughter you. You must be very careful.

PATRICK: You just watch me. I'm going to make my mark within society. Mr Devereux should start to count his days. I will not give up. He is responsible for destroying an innocent life.

CORAL: I'm so sorry you found out this way. I'm so sorry to have upset you (*picks up all the post*) I'm going to put this all back.

PETER: Wait, I haven't sealed that blue envelope yet!

ROSE: I just feel so bad for dear Patrick. It's so awful to find out bad news like this.

MEESHA: Rose, there never is a good time to find out bad news. It was something that was waiting to happen. And besides, if we hadn't told him, he would have found out another way.

ROSE: (*sighing*) I know, I know. I suppose I should be used to hearing terrible news, seeing as I'm working here. It's all run of the mill.

PETER: The oven's just buzzed, Rose.

ROSE: Yes, yes, it's all run of the mill. Anyone for cake?

All quietly continue to do their work. PETER *gets rid of the water and bowl, and* ROSE *opens the oven and takes out the sponge cake.*

SCENE SIX

THOMAS DEVEREUX *is at the cemetery. He is standing beside his mother's grave. Her tombstone reads, 'Forever Beautiful, forever kind, loved and missed dearly. Loni Beatrice Devereux – born 1937 – died 1964'.* THOMAS *places some flowers on the grave. He stares at the tomb for a little while then begins to talk to his mother. He kneels down, tidies his unkempt hair with his hands and straightens his clothing.*

THOMAS: Mummy, I had the most wonderful dream last night. I dreamt that you were still alive and well and Daddy hadn't beaten you or pushed you down the stairs. You had such a great smile. You seemed so peaceful. And then I saw you doing something rather odd. You were stroking something really sharp. Then I saw this shadow of a woman behind you. Quite a large shadow. I looked hard at it, I felt that I knew this stranger but I couldn't totally work out who she was. Before I could think any further, my peace was disrupted by one of our foolish maids. So I had to get up. It was only eleven o' clock in the morning! I do miss you, Mummy. I've done all sorts of things this week. I saw a fat pigeon in Aston Square and I chased it around until it flew away. Then I saw this big girl, she looked almost the same size as me. I winked at her and waved. She just walked away. Then I saw these lovely daffodils. I was trying to get some for you, but the owner saw me climbing over his fence and started shouting at me so I ran. Dad never gives you any flowers, does he? He's always too busy with something. He never really loved you, did he, Mummy? He just hurt you and then killed you. I really miss you, Mummy. I really do. I feel so lonely. I know I have the others. Penelope's always lovely, Nancy's a cow, I wish she was my stepsister, and Benjamin is a real brother to me. He understands my needs and he gives me money. Father always looks at me with daggers in his eyes. He never willingly gives me any money, so how am I supposed to cope? Auntie Sophie is all right most of the time. I secretly hate Veronica, though. I've never really liked the fact that she is my stepmother. If she were another aunt, I would be OK with that. Mummy, I've written a poem for you. Would you like to hear it? It's called 'The best mum in the world'. 'Dear Mummy, I miss you very much. Why did you have to leave this world so soon? I have cried floods of tears just for you. I miss your smile, your laughter, your cuddles and kisses. I miss those wonderful moments with you. I wish you were alive today. If only you could have stayed just with me. My life has never been the same. My life is in tatters. I love you Mummy, with all my heart. Please always look after me Mummy, because nobody else does.' Did you like that, Mummy? I hope you did. Mummy, do you watch over me? Do you know when I'm going to die? Is it soon? Will you greet me when I arrive at the gates? Can I stay with you? Then we can talk about everything. I hope I die soon so I can see you. There's no point in me living here. Nobody takes me seriously except Josie and Fleury. You'd like Fleury, Mummy. She's really funny and quite clever. She can balance a whole plate on the tip of her nose and it doesn't even wobble. She's also travelled quite a bit. She's been to America, France and Bhutan. She's also really bendy. She's a dancer. I never understand why women like to dance. Isn't it like exercising very fast with music? I don't know!

JOSIE *appears. She is slim, has long dark hair, is plain and of medium height. She slowly walks up to* THOMAS. *Once* THOMAS *notices* JOSIE, *his face lights up with a big smile.* JOSIE *reciprocates and quickly gives him a peck on the cheek.*

THOMAS: Josie, what are you doing here?
JOSIE: I was looking for you. I wanted to see you.
THOMAS: Did you get away from the fire all right? I would have saved you but I'm not very brave. I do not have much confidence.
JOSIE: Yes. I am fine. The bakery is in ashes, though. I don't have a job anymore.
THOMAS: I blame your buns. If they hadn't got burnt we would have been all right and I would have said a few more important things. Actually, I was going to talk to Mummy first about it. See if she approved and then tell you.
JOSIE: Is this your Mummy's grave?
THOMAS: Ah yes, let me introduce you. Mummy, this is Josie, Josie this is my Mummy. She loves me a lot and she takes good care of me.
JOSIE: Pleased to meet you, Mrs Devereux. Thomas tells me so many wonderful things about you. He speaks very highly of you.
THOMAS: Mummy, can I marry Josie? You know how much I love her and want to be with her. She likes me too.
JOSIE: (*flabbergasted*) What did you say?
THOMAS: I'm just checking with Mummy first and then I'll ask you. Can you please give me a second? It's very important she consents to this, otherwise if she says 'no' I'll have to stop seeing you.
JOSIE: Oh no! I don't want that to happen.
THOMAS: So let me talk to her first. Can you stand over there? (*He points to one side.*)

JOSIE *moves to one side and looks on as* THOMAS *continues.*

THOMAS: Mummy, I really love Josie. I know she will make a very pleasant wife. She understands my needs and she does listen to me and I'm sure you've noticed she is rather pretty. If you allow me to marry her I will go straight to her father and arrange the wedding and not invite anyone I know because everyone always criticises me. I suppose I could invite Ben. He could be my best man, the ring bearer, and also he could give me the money to do all this. I know I should invite Father, but he'll just yell at me. I'll have to buy a small cottage north of Fezaria-Aston and take Josie there. I do not want to live near my relatives. We can't stay in the mansion. I promise to stop drinking. I'll get Josie to hide the drinks or glue my lips or something. So what do you think, Mummy? That's my rough plan at the moment. You approve? Really? Oh, that is good news. I can't wait to tell Josie. Josie! Josie, you can come over now.

JOSIE *appears with tears in her eyes.*

THOMAS: Josie, I spoke to Mummy.
JOSIE: I know, I heard everything.
THOMAS: Now I'm going to pop the question.
JOSIE: Yes, yes, a hundred times yes.
THOMAS: Hang on. You don't know what I'm going to ask you yet!
JOSIE: Sorry! Sorry! (*She wipes her tears and begins to smile.*)
THOMAS: Josie McIntyre, will you please make me the most happiest man in the world and marry me?
JOSIE: Yes! Yes! A thousand times yes! (*She throws her arms open and hugs him tightly.*) I love you, Thomas Devereux. You cheeky little monkey!
THOMAS: Now ask me.
JOSIE: Pardon? I don't understand.
THOMAS: Ask me. I want to feel what you're feeling.
JOSIE: All right. Thomas Devereux, will you please make me the most happiest woman in the world and marry me?
THOMAS: Of course. I will my sweet. (*He too throws his arms open and as he hugs her he lifts her up in the air.*) You are the best thing that's ever happened to me. I love you with all my heart. And Mummy says you are absolutely gorgeous.

JOSIE: Oh thank you, Mrs Devereux.
THOMAS: I'm afraid it's not going to be a very swish wedding. You can invite all your family and I'll just invite Ben.
JOSIE: What about Penny? Don't you like her?
THOMAS: Yes I do, but Penny can't keep secrets. So no. She cannot come.
JOSIE: What about some of your cousins or Auntie Sophie? They like you, don't they?
THOMAS: Josie, I just can't have anyone there who's going to make me feel uncomfortable. And besides, I don't think they really care. They're too busy with their lives.
JOSIE: All right. Whatever makes you happy.
THOMAS: Did Mr Tunnell yell at you after the fire?
JOSIE: Yes, and then he let me go. He paid me two weeks wages. Never really liked working there anyway. Mr Tunnell was always bossing me around.
THOMAS: Well, at least you don't have to see him again.
JOSIE: I'd better be going now. I've got an interview with Mrs Meredith.
THOMAS: The florist?
JOSIE: Yes. She's looking for a bright and hard-working assistant. Worth a try, don't you think?
THOMAS: I'm sure you'll get the job, you're lovely.
JOSIE: Thank you. (*She kisses him*.)
THOMAS: Say goodbye to Mummy.
JOSIE: Goodbye, Mrs Devereux. I hope to see you again soon. Bye Thomas.
THOMAS: Bye sweetie.

JOSIE *merrily leaves the cemetery. Thomas stays on.*

THOMAS: Isn't she wonderful Mummy?

In a very relaxed mood, THOMAS *decides to lie down next to his mother's grave.*

SCENE SEVEN

JOHN BRASWICK *is anxiously seated in* FREDERICK DEVEREUX'S *bureau.* PENCHARD *is seated beside him. He watches him with a sharp eye.* JOHN *has been summoned by* FREDERICK *to attend an urgent meeting.* JOHN *is head of operations for one of the Devereux factories. He is in his early thirties, tall, fair and of medium build.* FREDERICK *is looking very closely at some paperwork and occasionally looking up at* JOHN.

FREDERICK: (*rather sternly*)   '... seriously hazardous, disturbing malfunction, unacceptable working conditions and extremely detrimental to any operator's health...' Have you read this, Braswick? Have you seen this startling report? Do you fully comprehend the assessment made by the inspectors?

JOHN: I have read...

FREDERICK: Do you know what all this means? It means we are running a very incompetent, reckless and wicked business. This means our factories are the most dangerous environments to work in. In this particular case, at FD008, we have 329 members of staff, of which six are in management, and you, Mr Braswick, are in charge of all operations verifying the company machinery and making certain that any repairs needed are carried out securely. Is that correct?

JOHN: Yes, yes, that is correct but...

FREDERICK: I have been informed there is a great deal of maladministration, countless blunders resulting in three members of staff becoming injured, not to forget one unfortunate chap who was almost killed due to faulty mechanics. What do you have to say about that?

JOHN: We have been facing specific difficulties…

FREDERICK: I don't want to hear it! Never have I had to speak to someone like you before who seems to have no idea of the fatal consequences following negligent practices at work. Never have I had the horrific pleasure of speaking to someone so blindly out of touch with the world of common sense. And never have I had to tolerate such disparaging and derogatory reports about the businesses I run. Low profit margin is one thing but to lose out due to a pathetic, ill-educated member of staff who has no knowledge of the workplace is quite unpardonable in my opinion.

JOHN: Mr Devereux, sir, you promised my father that…

FREDERICK: Your father totally misled me. He sincerely assured me that you had the appropriate capabilities to run approved checks on FD008 machinery. He gave me firm assurance that not only do you have the apposite knowledge but amazing ideas on how to further the company's potential. My goodness me, I thought I was in very capable hands. I didn't know your father was a liar! A father always thinks very highly of his children but what he appears to forget is that society – especially those who are not related – has the natural ability to scrutinise and judge vehemently. The apple of one's eye becomes a thorn for others.

JOHN: Sir, you have said quite enough! If you wish to fire me then please summon my father first. Let's see what he thinks of this. I'm certain that he will not allow you to get rid of me. Your machinery is antiquated. If you do not cease production for even a few hours then how are the repairmen going to diagnose the problem and fix it? If making money is always, paramount regardless of other alarming factors then, yes, the report before your very eyes is inevitable. I, on many occasions, tried my best to stop production, but your faithful nuisance, Penchard, prohibited any stoppage of operation.

Penchard seemed to know it all and the rest of us in the factory and office were only making up the numbers.
PENCHARD: Sir, I beg to differ. That is absolutely not true! I did try to help whenever possible. I never disallowed any proper repairs.
JOHN: Penchard, you are blatantly lying. When Mr Devereux is not around, you appear to assume that your presence is of greater superiority. You look down at everyone else. You show no respect to fellow employees!
PENCHARD: Mr John Braswick, do not digress to petty personal issues.
FREDERICK: Penchard is correct. There were instances where I was very tolerant towards your working demeanour. Now I am afraid that you have overstayed your welcome, Mr Braswick.
JOHN: I do not accept your terms at all. You are dismissing me because you simply have no one else to blame. Now things have gone wrong due to your dismissive attitude, I am the lucky scapegoat. Bravo! How unspeakably fair you both are!
FREDERICK: Please do give my regards to your father. He is of course still very welcome to attend the Dex this year.
JOHN: What about notice of dismissal? You must give me sufficient notice before you ask me to leave.
FREDERICK: Do you know who I am, Mr Braswick? Let me remind you. I am Frederick Charles Devereux. I have and am responsible for one of the greatest lucrative business empires possible. Within that dynamic sphere, I apply my own personal rules. I have particular methods that are only brilliant to those who genuinely appreciate me as a worthy humanitarian. You, my boy, have succeeded in spotting your fragile and bitter weaknesses and have decided to take that discoloured anger out on me.
JOHN: That is total and utter rubbish and you know it, Mr Devereux! You have absolutely no idea how to treat people, especially your own staff. You are full of ludicrous talk that

not only torments people but also confirms how tyrannical you are. Please do not tell me how I think. I quit! My father shall be in touch. I thought he mentioned you were great friends. He must have meant great enemies. Penchard, try and take your head out of Mr Devereux's bottom. You might get a better picture of life.

PENCHARD: How dare you!

JOHN: I just did. Any money owing, please forward it to my humble abode.

FREDERICK: Your father is rich, that's why I know him. No other reason for acquiring his friendship. The door is wide open. You may leave me now and any further discourse, I will make absolutely certain that all other job opportunities are closed to you.

JOHN: You can't do that!

FREDERICK: Oh, I definitely have the power to do that and come to think of it I will, except, of course, for employment here. I will leave opportunities open for you here because when you have looked for work, you will have searched high and low until you come to my doorstep once more. Since you will need work, you will shamefully hang your head in front of me and ask for your job back. Seeing that, I will take great pleasure in stripping, very finely, your self-confidence, your naïve beliefs in the world, and will successfully use you until I become rather bored.

JOHN: People like you should be buried alive or better still burnt alive!

FREDERICK: I await your desperate return and I will save the wicked laughter till last. Penchard, please escort Mr John Braswick out of the mansion and then burn all damaging paperwork.

PENCHARD: Certainly sir! Come along now, Braswick.

PENCHARD *holds* BRASWICK*'s arm tightly and takes him out of the room.* BRASWICK *gives* MR DEVEREUX *a very evil look as he reluctantly walks away.* FREDERICK *remains motionless.*

SCENE EIGHT

NANCY *is at the railway station awaiting the arrival of a friend. After a few moments a tall dark figure appears, wrapped up in a winter fur.* NANCY *is meeting* MISHTY SHAKAR. *She has a strong American accent. She alights the train with a small brown suitcase.*

MISHTY: You call this public transportation? The seats are too uncomfortable and the doors are too heavy to open with one hand. Hello? Has anyone heard of automatic doors? The train driver must consume alcohol for breakfast and have an attitude about velocity. I do not have insurance to claim on for a crooked and punched-up hat! I just chipped a nail and my manicure is in New York. I thought smoking was not allowed on your trains. That stupid ugly-looking wafer of a rat must have been smoking for the entire nation of the United Kingdom! Now my hair smells, my coat's ruined and if the train had not stopped at this point I would have been gasping for a nebuliser! I didn't bother with any insurance, so God knows how I would have paid for any medical treatment. My heels have had enough. The flight was OK, though. The food was edible and the entertainment allowed me to sleep for hours.
NANCY: Welcome to Fezaria-Aston.
MISHTY: Before we get started I need a hairdresser. Too many altitudes have rocked the great bouffant style of an elegant lady.
NANCY: I have the perfect venue for you.
MISHTY: Good! So what's been happening?
NANCY: The letter arrived. She's absolutely besotted.

MISHTY: But you're happy with what I've done so far?
NANCY: Yes. You have completely destroyed his quality of life in the US. Now we need to come up with another plan that will undeniably leave Daniel destitute here as well.
MISHTY: What's he doing now?
NANCY: Penny is meeting him at the Cerissia Hotel on Tuesday. I'm assuming he is going to grovel and plead until she takes him back.
MISHTY: The little mutinous toad is playing that game again. He's going to wipe her out. He is broke, period. The clothes that he is wearing are stolen. His shoes are from the streets of the Bronx and his tired and beaten face is hiding under the mask he is wearing now. The IRS have been all over me. Luckily, Chippy Tuchovski, my handsome young friend, baled me out. He spoke to the big cheese and now everything is cool. Has my lipstick smeared?
NANCY: No, it's fine.
MISHTY: Could we get a cup of coffee or something? I really need some caffeine.
NANCY: Max should be waiting for us. We'll go to the 'Grapple' on the way to the cottage.
MISHTY: Oh, thanks for the cheque by the way. It came in handy when securing a property in the Caribbean, which you're welcome to stay in whenever you wish.
NANCY: Useful to know. Did Angela find Crane before you left?
MISHTY: Yes. Crane was in Houston, Texas. Angela was worried sick.
NANCY: At least we found him.
MISHTY: The access codes are in his pocket and the authorities are waiting for him in South Dakota.
NANCY: Why exactly?
MISHTY: He harmed a woman and her family. They laughed at his walk and pointed rudely.
NANCY: Oh dear! He must have flipped.

MISHTY: Almost over the top. It took four men to calm him down.
NANCY: I wouldn't expect anything less.
MISHTY: His friend Jobo, in Texas, said he would help him out. The situation is rather sensitive.
NANCY: Do you think he'll be all right?
MISHTY: If you're worried about the access codes, don't be. We're talking about Crane. He'll make it. He's invincible. No other human being can get in his way.
NANCY: I have been waiting for those access codes for years.
MISHTY: It still astonishes me how you went in for a drink at a bar and two hours later you came out with elephantine wealth.
NANCY: He was playing around with his drink and annoying the barmaid. She repeatedly told him to behave, but Crane acted even more like a delinquent. Finally, his uncontrollable rage hit its zenith and he was ready to throw a large bottle of whisky at her, but fortunately I had the power and good sense to stop him.
MISHTY: Right after that he was imprisoned. I think it was attempted murder.
NANCY: But of course I got him out of prison. He fitted my criteria to qualify as a skilful and astute member of our group, and after a little financial aid and some sweet charm the authorities released him.
MISHTY: Sometimes he scares me.
NANCY: We all have our unique abilities. Now, let's see how it all works out. Angela and Crane will join us and we shall gather to take on our borrowed identities at the Dex. The secondary plan will certainly mark the end of an era.
MISHTY: Are you absolutely confident about your scheme?
NANCY: Confrontation is a great taste. I will blindly blame and shout and exploit my fierce tone until I am ready.
MISHTY: Do you think it's a good idea for anyone to hear your voice? That might become a refreshing lead in the murder investigation.

NANCY: I was not born a coward. I want the glorious moment to tremble at my words, I want him to feel the fear. You will all be prepared for the exit. Keep a vigil, and after I watch his blood drain away, I will happily embrace his departure and welcome unlimited wealth and pure indulgence with open arms. I simply cannot wait. The enchanting hour has become my permanent dream.

MISHTY: Doesn't he call you his 'angel'?

NANCY: Angel is just a word. An incentive for me to be well mannered in a sinister way. You must not always associate good with angels. I do not understand why I cannot automatically be entitled to my share. Why do I have to wait until his demise? I am ready now.

MISHTY: Crane says that you should kill him in one stab and forget about using the access codes. Even if your megabytes give you sound entry to the millions, your father will find out and hammer you down.

NANCY: Not necessarily. I anticipate certain complications, but in the end I will be triumphant.

MISHTY: I'll drink to that.

NANCY: Astuteness is the greatest compliment you can receive. If you apply astuteness with surprise, you will have reached your peak and nobody will have the intellect to ever suspect you. The mere thought of escaping guilt and imprisonment is thrilling.

MISHTY: Crane calls it sophistication.

NANCY: Mishty, all four of us will set a new vogue in the world of crime.

MISHTY: As long as I get my cut, I'm happy!

NANCY: £74 million is a lot to get happy about.

They continue to walk.

SCENE NINE

VERONICA *and* FREDERICK *are resting in their luxurious bedroom. They are sitting up in bed. He has some paperwork in his hand.* VERONICA *is cross.*

FREDERICK: The Richmonds cannot make it to the Dex this year, can you believe it?
VERONICA: Oh.
FREDERICK: You don't seem very concerned.
VERONICA: I thought we were going to celebrate later.
FREDERICK: What are you talking about, woman?
VERONICA: My birthday. I thought you said we were going to celebrate later?
FREDERICK: Ah yes! Naturally. That was only a line. You know, something that you wanted to hear. I thought I might say it to make you feel that little bit special.
VERONICA: Oh, how kind of you, sire!
FREDERICK: There is simply no need to get upset. It's only one day.
VERONICA: I was hoping for a better response than that.
FREDERICK: Look, I am a very busy man. If you hadn't noticed, I normally have a hundred and one things to do. I run a very big empire. If my daily routine has to be disturbed for a pointless cause then I would rather keep that frivolous event at bay.
VERONICA: Why does this year have to be different? We celebrated my birthday last year.
FREDERICK: Last year is a very good reason not to celebrate it this year and the next one and so on. Anyway, this year I had already forgotten until Meesha happened to mention it. That is why I decided to use that line in front of Sophie.

VERONICA: Why does it have to be so complicated?
FREDERICK: If you are after a gift of some sort I am sure your weekly allowance will come in handy. Why don't you summon one of the chauffeurs and go out of town. Go and purchase a pair of earrings or something. Don't they say jewellery is a woman's best friend?
VERONICA: I have earrings.
FREDERICK: Must you keep on!

There is a knock at the door. CORAL *appears with a tray in her hand. She enters and places two cups of cocoa on the table at the foot of the bed.*

VERONICA: Thank you, Coral.
CORAL: It is a little bit hot, so please do wait a little while before you drink it.
FREDERICK: We can see perfectly that both drinks are hot, we have no intention of burning our mouths. That will be all, Coral. Please make sure you shut the door properly on your way out.
VERONICA: Is Meesha on duty tomorrow?
CORAL: I am not sure, ma'am. Would you like me to check?
VERONICA: No, don't worry about it. I thought she might want to have a look at another old outfit before I gave it away.
CORAL: Ma'am, could I possibly have a look? I do always notice how well you dress.
VERONICA: Of course! Why not! Remind me tomorrow morning. All right?
CORAL: Oh thank you so much!
FREDERICK: Coral, it is getting rather late. Please leave.
CORAL: Sorry, sir.

She exits quietly but remains excited.

VERONICA: I completely forgot that your middle name was disappointment.
FREDERICK: My goodness me, you are a miserable beast!
VERONICA: That's why Benjamin is never able to relate to you! You always seem to turn a blind eye to all his needs.
FREDERICK: I know what his needs are, I am his father, although I do have suspicions about your maternal role.
VERONICA: I am a very good mother. I know when my son is unhappy, I know when he's pleased. And I certainly know when it's his birthday.
FREDERICK: You are a very unusual creature. You do not understand what the world is about.
VERONICA: I wish I had a better way of living! You keep jabbing hostile feelings towards me. Sometimes I just cannot deal with them.
FREDERICK: The last twenty-five years should have sorted you out.
VERONICA: Every time I reason with you, you always try too push me away. You always want me to accept anything and everything as it is. Don't you ever think about me?
FREDERICK: My future depends entirely upon the decisions I make. The decision can only be made when I have a cool head. With a wife and son sometimes that coolness escapes me. I find thorns within my decisions. I become rather exasperated and almost hopeless. But the question is why? You seem to be eating my brain away. Could you please stop?
VERONICA: I need to live my life too, you know.
FREDERICK: You can do whatever you like provided I know what is going on.
VERONICA: I wanted to learn how to drive, I wanted to learn dressmaking and I wanted to set up my own fashion shop, but oh no, you wouldn't let me.
FREDERICK: Your recreational interests worry me a great deal. You are determined to show poor taste in whichever

field you are keen on. From the very first day I met you I knew you would not have that majestic spirit. You were painfully shy and you proved to know very little. I remember when we went out to a grand hotel, I think it was the Mox, you kept gaping at the decor and you were so attentive towards the waiting staff. And you were all fingers and thumbs when it came to using the cutlery.

VERONICA: If I was so inadequate then why did you even look at me? Why didn't you let me stay on the shelf until some average rogue came along?

FREDERICK: Loni died in terrible circumstances and then I needed a nanny more than anything else and if I ended up having a child or two it would not be a problem. My elitist instinct would obviously see to any additional expenditure.

VERONICA: You're hardly the husband I thought you would be. You don't love me, you just tag me along and I just follow like a stupid ass.

FREDERICK: What can I say! You have to pay the price for being underprivileged. If your father had been rich and glorious and had truly made a name for himself within society you would certainly have had more choices, my dear. More pleasant choices indeed.

VERONICA: When I first arrived at this mansion, I asked for a new pair of shoes. You made me wear all of Loni's shoes. They weren't even the right size.

FREDERICK: That hardly matters! And besides your feet must have felt privileged to be in those top quality shoes.

VERONICA: Your wicked manner reduces me to tears. I do not deserve unhappiness.

FREDERICK: Your naïve manner reduces me to exasperation. Women know how to cry beautifully, but ask them to think and generate power and use it effectively, they quiver like leaves.

VERONICA: You are entirely responsible for taking my livelihood away. In the beginning I thought was in good hands.

FREDERICK: Are you not used to the Devereux approach to living? Your only commitment to me is to act like my wife. You certainly do not have the fervent quality of being my wife. Loni has always been my true and loving wife.

VERONICA: Some people think she is still alive.

FREDERICK: What a ridiculous thing to say! You must have a chemical imbalance or in your old age you are approaching senility. She is dead and her funeral was a very traumatic event to absorb. I may not show my inner feelings but they are ones of pain and disbelief. Sometimes I look at Thomas and Penelope and I see her. It crushes me.

VERONICA: And to think I actually believed you were capable of loving me.

FREDERICK: Money draws people together. Love is a single moment searching desperately for an enchanting flash of passion. Money saves you from that sort of embarrassment.

VERONICA: Love is not something that is born overnight. It has to be a natural feeling embodied with trust and contentment.

FREDERICK: Elitism has always been the best step forward. Even if you do turn your nose up at it, elitism can work wonders. People go out of their way to throw themselves at you. They always are aware that you have something they do not. If elitism is supposed to be such a bad thing then why do people become jealous?

VERONICA: Could you see if there are any headache tablets in your top drawer please?

FREDERICK: Just as I am coming to something meaningful you have decided to use the oldest trick in the book. Don't you associate headaches with sex?

VERONICA: Wow! You actually know the word 'sex'! Do you know how to perform? No. Of course not.

FREDERICK: (*He draws out a packet of tablets and throws them onto her lap.*) Sex is for youngsters. Our age makes us far too old to engage in that sort of thing.

VERONICA: I know I have long suffered with my hormones. They are in a dire state. You have had no lust for me since Benjamin was six years of age.
FREDERICK: Six years was long enough. Desire in a man can only last so many years for one woman. Especially his second wife.
VERONICA: (*She throws the tablets in her mouth and washes them down with a glass of water.*) The fact is, you do not find me attractive anymore but I find you very alluring. (*She reaches out for his leg.*)
FREDERICK: Could you please let go.
VERONICA: I was hoping that would set some testosterone racing.
FREDERICK: Let me put you in your place. I find great pleasure in looking at other women.
VERONICA: So what do they do that is different?
FREDERICK: I have a considerable amount of paperwork left to do. These won't finish themselves you know.
VERONICA: I hear many stories about your discreet little visits to posh hotels and your unsightly frolics with innocent young girls. I have never put you on the spot and demanded full answers about them but I would certainly like to hear some sort of explanation concerning your misbehaviour.
FREDERICK: There are times when high-ranking and heavily moneyed professionals like me have to take a break. This is what I choose to do. I do not like silly questions and I will not give accurate answers because discussing all this is a waste of valuable time. I wish to move on.
VERONICA: Don't you understand how immoral your methods are?
FREDERICK: If you wish to have a roof over your head then stop getting on my nerves.
VERONICA: Kenneth has contacted me again, asking if I want to join the social spectrum group. I wish you would let me say yes. It is such a wonderful opportunity to mix with other

people and enjoy one another's company and do something decent for the community.

FREDERICK: I will not permit you to rub shoulders with the bourgeoisie.

VERONICA: They are the most interesting people in society.

FREDERICK: Because they are needy. These are mortals who are constantly overshadowed by us.

VERONICA: You still forgot my birthday.

FREDERICK: Happy birthday, Veronica. Many happy returns. Now, pass me my pen and go to sleep.

VERONICA: My headache won't let me.

FREDERICK: I wonder if there is medication that will stop you talking gibberish.

VERONICA: Could I at least go to the Pierce and Bright charity event on Tuesday?

FREDERICK: Of course. There will be hundreds of affluent people and trays of caviar. Need you ask?

VERONICA: How much money can I spend?

FREDERICK: Up to £325,000. No more than that. Please make sure you know what you are doing. Be careful not to show your real roots. Many can sense very easily that you were not born with a silver spoon in your mouth.

VERONICA: Frederick Devereux, I do have experience. I am able to pull it off.

FREDERICK: Your not-so-polished nature makes me nervous. That is why I choose not to accompany you to certain important events.

VERONICA: How sweet my fate is.

FREDERICK: Benjamin was a divine gift from God. He sent him to appease me. Marriage is a necessary ceremony that gives you respect and a commendable status amongst your peers. After that, with time, unevenness settles in. In order to rescue yourself from the depths of irregularity you require a new interest. An heir.

VERONICA: I do not want to be an elitist, I do not want to be unnaturally fierce and I do not wish to be a phoney. I have always believed in being myself.

FREDERICK: I am the commander here. I am the one who knows best. Are you insinuating that you doubt my capabilities in making a suitable decision?

VERONICA: I doubt that you actually know yourself. I doubt that you understand others around you and I doubt that you will ever know what is real.

FREDERICK: How dare you!

VERONICA: I must go to sleep now. I have an early day tomorrow. Goodnight, Frederick. I hope the paperwork keeps you up all night.

FREDERICK: You know very little. I know that.

VERONICA: I might go to my parents for a while. I haven't seen them for weeks.

FREDERICK: When you do see them, could you tell your brother to clear the last cheque I gave him. I wrote the damn thing out four weeks ago and still there has been no withdrawal.

VERONICA: Maybe he's forgotten.

FREDERICK: If he does not take the funds by tomorrow, I will stop the cheque.

VERONICA: I'll tell him to do it as soon as possible. Why I can't just offer them money from my allowance, I don't know. It makes sense that way, surely?

FREDERICK: If I write the cheques, then I know how much is going out and I can keep an eye on what your family are spending. I do not want them costing me a small fortune, now do I?

VERONICA: A thousand pounds a month for a family of six is hardly enough! They have a lot of requirements.

FREDERICK: People who live by another's means have no hold over what they need or do not need. There may be a day when I do not want to write out a cheque. There may be a day where I will write one cheque after another and then simply cancel every single one of them if your brother or any other member of your family irritates me in the slightest. I have the power to do this. Your family was born powerless and lacks authority. They are living on borrowed means. Their voice is mute. Let me guide them as I please.

VERONICA: I wish I could walk out on you.

FREDERICK: That day will never come, Veronica.

VERONICA: I wish I was loved.

FREDERICK: You will be. The angels like straight-laced women.

VERONICA: Do you ever think about killing me? Maybe putting me to rest gracefully?

FREDERICK: The gracious thought did occur to me.

VERONICA: Do you hate me?

FREDERICK: You are the mother of one of my children, I am not allowed to hate you.

VERONICA: So what on earth do you feel towards me?

FREDERICK: That is a puzzle at the moment. I am sure Penchard will be able to think of something deep and meaningful for your ears only.

VERONICA: How reassuring!

FREDERICK: Benjamin seems to have inherited most of his stubborn ways from you.

VERONICA: He just wants what makes him happy. Any mother is able to see that. The major problem is that you will not allow him to be joyful because his tastes clash with yours.

FREDERICK: The boy needs discipline.

VERONICA: The boy needs a father.

FREDERICK: He needs a good hiding.

VERONICA: Violence never solves anything.

FREDERICK: Depends how you use the magnificent tool.

VERONICA: Yes. Quite. It is second nature for you, isn't it?

FREDERICK: Only an essential tool. It is not something I aim toward automatically. Any action is provoked.

VERONICA: I sincerely believe you are wrong.
FREDERICK: I sincerely believe that you should shut up.
VERONICA: I must get some sleep. My eyes are very tired.

FREDERICK *begins to shuffle through his paperwork.*

SCENE TEN

Much to FREDERICK*'s annoyance, after tossing and turning,* VERONICA *finally falls into a deep sleep.* BENJAMIN *appears.*

BENJAMIN: You call yourself a mother? What kind of a mother are you? I am going through such a tough time and here you are by my callous and selfish father's side, echoing his grotesque and hurtful words. Do you care about me? I thought I was your only child? I thought I was special? Why are you tormenting me like this? I cry so much for your love and attention. Why do you seem busy with other things? Do you not love me anymore? Am I that awful to you? Father has no idea about my feelings and he does not care how he hurts me. As long as he gets his own way, everything to him is perfect. I wish I were dead. I wish I had been born into a proper, loving, caring and appreciative family. I appear to be a nobody. Thank you for giving me life and thank you for not listening to me. You seem well suited to this family. Michelle always understood me. She was my best friend. She always looked at me with loving eyes. I miss her very much. Michelle did not fear anyone. She was always an honest person. She never lied to me. She was grateful to have met me. And so what if I helped her out by giving her money. It was always a privilege. She was the one to make me feel happy. She was the one to make me feel secure. She never had a complaint. She never doubted me. I was in love and I still am. Even though she had difficulty reading complicated words and did not comprehend all aspects of our lifestyle, she never was shy to admit it. She was a genuine role model. I wish people knew more about her. She gave me strength and she gave me hope. All that has vanished now. I feel lost. I cannot heal these wounds. Time may be a great healer but that time has not passed. I feel bitter and bewildered. Thomas is the fortunate and very wise one. He only looks through intoxicated glasses and so has no idea about reality. I should follow in his footsteps. That way I will feel no pain and there will be no more questions.

BENJAMIN *fades away and then suddenly* SOPHIE *appears.*

SOPHIE: I applaud you for being such an unfit and despondent mother. You have no awareness of your responsibilities and you certainly do not understand the regime of this family. You are not of good grain. Your head holds degenerate thoughts. I regret meeting you. I cannot believe that I have to walk on the same ground as you. I cannot believe that I even have to look at you. You have been born with a small-minded nature. You have qualities I look for in our maids. If there had been an application form for the position of head sweeper I am sure you would have been successful. A sweeper always has his head down and has the benefit of staring at the floor. The world is not your oyster, therefore the position would have fitted you perfectly. Your life has no meaning and you are just filling a role that unfortunately needs to be filled. You are nothing, Veronica. You are the laughing stock of Fezaria-Aston. I hate you. You disgust me. You're a prosaic creature. You lack vivacity. You are not a decent mother. You will never be a decent mother. Never! Never! Never!

As SOPHIE *turns her back,* NANCY *walks forward looking straight at her.*

NANCY: Roses are red, violets are blue, Benjamin is in a mess and we all blame you! Hello stepmother. How was your day?

Was it wonderful? Was it enjoyable? Or was it pitiful and grey? You are the new messenger of danger, you are the bearer of total despair. Benjamin is perturbed and heartbroken, but what do you care? You are dressed up like a mannequin with synthetic intelligence. Congratulations on your new role, we all look at you with abhorrence. You will never be accepted as part of the Devereux family. You are still here because of my father's money. You are not real, you are a joke. Your appearance, your stature, your language scare other folk. Please kindly pack your cases and quietly leave, for then we can celebrate and finally grieve. Benjamin is very unlucky to have you as his mother, although I personally feel that he is closer to me than my own brother. The door is wide open, take your exit. Do not look back, do not feign any tears. We will release the joyful banners and let out enormous cheers.

NANCY *takes a bow and then waves farewell. When she stops* FREDERICK *emerges.*

FREDERICK: Money! Money! Money! That is all I ever wanted. Money! Money! Money! That is all I ever dreamed of. I love money and I love myself, but who are you? Who let you in? My life is surrounded with large banknotes. My heart is a fixed crest of sterling. A wife has no place within my heart. You expect me to love you? That is impossible. I only love money. I worship it. I revere it. I gladly embrace it. I adore it. I do not have time for you. Your family wastes enough of my time and money. I wish the tedious treaty would come to an end so that I would not have to pay them any longer. I want the contract to disappear. I wish I could strangle every single member of your family but I suppose I cannot disable you like that. After all, my foolishness made me agree to pay them for as long as we are married. Perhaps I should divorce you? But I'm a successful man, I cannot do that. You are lucky to have a son. You are lucky that I allowed you to have a child because I truly find you an eyesore. So please turn the other way. The girls that entertain me are more appealing than you will ever be. I do not believe in love, I just believe in fun and games and spending my own money. It would be quite immoral of me to lock you up in a cage. Although sometimes I feel it would be necessary. There are days when I wish you would not wake up. There are days when I wish you would gracefully retire. On hearing your passing I will thank the Lord without shedding a single tear. I will only remember you as Benjamin's deranged and incompetent mother.

FREDERICK *continues but his words become inaudible. His figure begins to shrink and gradually another figure comes into view. This is a* FEMININE FIGURE *in the form of a silhouette. She has a bright smile, a very pleasant face and approaches* VERONICA *with a very hospitable demeanour. She initiates her speech.*

FEMININE FIGURE: Don't listen to any of them. You are a magnificent person. You have immense patience and profound wisdom. You have the gift of being true to yourself. You have no fear about reality and your continuing courage shows. You speak your mind boldly and you care about the ones around you. You are a worthy mother. You do not cause nasty conflict. You have aged charmingly and put up with the Devereux family very well. You shall be rewarded, Veronica Mary Devereux. You will receive an exceptional bounty, thanks to somebody else's doing. Do not worry, the dawdling seconds will pass, the ominous minutes will press on, and the strenuous hours will fly. And finally the gruelling days will be over and then you will find real happiness. Your headaches will vanish. You will be victorious and no one will be seen on the same pedestal as you. You will acquire colossal wealth and your prime status will become the cause of envy. I commend you, my dear, your incredible endurance is ineffable. You shall be triumphant because you have always been faithful. Your shoulders will have no more unpromising burdens and your own family will support you even more. Just remember, Frederick Devereux will not harass you for long. His days are numbered. Now sleep well, my dear Veronica. Be peaceful within. Tomorrow is another day.

VERONICA *suddenly wakes up in a cold sweat. She gasps for air. She takes a look around her room. Everything is still and* FREDERICK *is fast asleep.*

SCENE ELEVEN

The Cerissia Hotel. One of the most prestigious in town. DANIEL SULLIVAN, *in his late thirties, very tall, dark and very handsome, is nervously awaiting* PENELOPE*'s arrival. He is very smartly dressed in blue. He is walking up and down the hotel reception area with a bouquet of red roses. His eyes are fixed on the mahogany double-door entrance. Every time someone comes in he looks up very sharply, but there is no sign of* PENELOPE. *The large hotel clock chimes twelve.* PENELOPE *is late. The double doors open once more and as* DANIEL *jumps up and quickly tries to look again, he clumsily knocks over one of the guests' bags.* DANIEL *apologises profusely and as he turns he accidentally walks into someone. It is* PENELOPE. PENELOPE *looks radiant in her sky-blue outfit and navy-blue shawl. She looks very elegant.* DANIEL *looks straight at her with relief and amazement.* PENELOPE *moves closer to him, stares very hard for a few seconds, and then she speaks. Throughout the whole conversation they maintain strong eye contact.*

PENELOPE: You're still too handsome, Daniel.
DANIEL: I thought you weren't going to come. I was so worried. These are for you (*handing the roses to her*).
PENELOPE: (*She does not take them.*) Regrettably, a wasted gesture! You're very kind, but no thank you. I'm glad you were worried. Shall we sit?

As PENELOPE *takes a seat,* DANIEL, *a little flummoxed, puts the roses on the floor and then swiftly sits beside her.*

DANIEL: I'm very delighted that you read my letter.

PENELOPE: Very long-winded letter. I felt like throwing it away.
DANIEL: But you didn't.
PENELOPE: I like to think I am fair when considering people's feelings. So I decided to give you the benefit of the doubt. I decided to give you a chance to prove to me in no uncertain terms that the language in your letter is absolutely genuine.
DANIEL: Thank you so much. You don't know how wonderful...
PENELOPE: When did you arrive back from New York?
DANIEL: Ten days ago. I was due to return earlier but I was busy trying to sell the house and business. Unfortunately, fate has not been on my side so the banks took everything from me. Now I have nothing to my name.
PENELOPE: What about your furniture business here?
DANIEL: I sold that to set up my life in America.
PENELOPE: Don't you have any friends? Surely they could have helped you out?
DANIEL: No. I had friends that I could never trust.
PENELOPE: Then they're really not friends, are they?
DANIEL: Can I get you anything? A drink of some sort?
PENELOPE: Calm down, Daniel. Why are you so tense? Relax. This is going to be less painful than you think.
PENELOPE: So tell me, where are you staying?
DANIEL: At the moment I am lodging at the Rickman's Inn. I am looking for temporary accommodation.
PENELOPE: Are you here on a permanent basis?
DANIEL: Yes. Most definitely. If I return to America, the IRS sharks will only want to sink their teeth into me. I still owe quite a bit of money.
PENELOPE: What a funny story.
DANIEL: That's why I was in hospital for a few days before leaving the country. I was terribly depressed.
PENELOPE: (*sarcastically*)   I'm so sorry to hear that. Wasn't there anyone by your side as you were suffering the sting of debt?

DANIEL: You mean Mishty? No, she and I have gone our separate ways.
PENELOPE: Do you still love her?
DANIEL: I hate her with all my heart. Believe me, Penny, I regretted marrying her from the very beginning, but once the wedding was over I didn't know how to turn back. I always thought about you. Even though I was married to her I felt rather lonely. She was too busy with her life and I seemed to get in her way.
PENELOPE: I never really thought about you. I was too busy setting up my own life and furthering my career. I didn't want to drown in despair.
DANIEL: Good for you.
PENELOPE: So what would you like to do now? Kiss and make up? Now that you have lost everything I seem to be the only hope left.
DANIEL: Yes. You are my only hope.
PENELOPE: Well, the fact of the matter is there is nothing I can do about it, Daniel. I have moved on and I have finally come to a place in my life where there is simply no room for you.
DANIEL: I understand. (*Pause*) But I love you. I've always loved you. Mishty and America were the biggest mistakes of my life.
PENELOPE: Do you have any children?
DANIEL: No. Mishty had a miscarriage. She was very upset.
PENELOPE: So what are your plans? You know, after meeting with me and not getting anywhere. What were you thinking of doing?
DANIEL: Getting a job somewhere and then contacting my parents. I haven't spoken to them in a while.
PENELOPE: Did you really kill your brother?
DANIEL: No. I just helped him with his dying wish.
PENELOPE: People still say that you are to blame for his demise.
DANIEL: I was close to him. The pain that he was feeling

affected me as well. He said that he would never forgive me if I continued to let him waste away. He made me promise to help him reach his peace. So I obliged. I agreed with him.
PENELOPE: Haven't your parents accepted that yet?
DANIEL: No. They hate me and so does my sister. Every time I ring her she cuts me off. She thinks I'm a murderer too.
PENELOPE: Do you think you're a murderer?
DANIEL: I am a brother who helped out his sibling in his hour of need. I do not need to think about justifying my actions. I believe I am right and that's what counts. There is no guilt, just sorrow. Just sheer remorse at not being able to share my life with him anymore. I loved him dearly. America was a way of trying to put all this behind me.
PENELOPE: Did you steal from my father?
DANIEL: No, of course not. It was all a complete misunderstanding. I had found these large wads of fifty-pound notes in a grey bag within the mansion. So naturally I decided to find Frederick and hand them to him, but then I found myself walking in on Nancy and Penchard purely by mistake. They were startled. Nancy hurriedly did up her shirt and composed her hair. Penchard was mortified. He was trying to get rid of Nancy's cherry-colour lipstick. I apologised immediately but Penchard snapped at me and Nancy began to question me harshly. She was utterly rude but I think she acted in that manner because of what I had seen. Why would I steal money when I had my own? I was only trying to do the right thing.
PENELOPE: Wait a minute! Did you say Penchard and Nancy? They were together in Father's bureau?
DANIEL: Yes. They were all over each other.
PENELOPE: Well I never! She swore that there was nothing going on. She said that I was making a childish remark. She said I was being silly. After that I thought nothing of it. I knew there was a rumour going around but I honestly didn't think it would be true.

DANIEL: Oh, I am sorry. Did I just let the cat out of the bag?
PENELOPE: My God! She's crazy! Of all people, Penchard!
DANIEL: It was so unfortunate. The money must have been there for a while. I was puzzled by...
PENELOPE: Daniel, you don't have to explain any further.
DANIEL: Is there anything else that you would like to ask me? Anything you want. I really don't mind.
PENELOPE: Do you really love me?
DANIEL: Every sinew in my body utters your name. It's as if I have you under my skin. I yearn for your loving attention, Penny. I need you more than ever.
PENELOPE: So if I decide to refuse you, you will be all right with that, will you?
DANIEL: If that is what you have decided after reading my letter and meeting with me then I have no choice but to accept that. I will miss you. There were so many times when I wanted to pick up the phone and just talk to you until it was bedtime. I missed hearing your voice. I missed being with you. I suppose I am the victim of my foolish decisions.
PENELOPE: I have been missing you since the day you walked out on me. I wanted to do so much, but your greed and determination to flee the country to our detriment truly wounded me. To this day you will have no idea how much, but naturally that is all in the past.
DANIEL: I think of you all the time. I have loved you and I still madly love you, and if it isn't too much to ask I would occasionally like to meet with you as friends only. I wouldn't ask any more of you if that is what you want.
PENELOPE: Good! I'm pleased that you understand this in a different but very favourable manner. You seem to be on the same wavelength as me. Thank you for your kindness. Oh; by the way, that precious letter has become an exclusive dartboard for the mansion staff. Not only did they read it and laugh at all hours of the morning, I found myself totally

drunk with hysteria and the next day two maids dragged me to my bedroom and helped me get sober.

DANIEL: I thought you didn't drink.

PENELOPE: That letter made it possible. Your repentance and affection were the laughing stock of the Devereux mansion.

DANIEL: I see. So I'm really wasting my time.

PENELOPE: The door is over there. Once you're on the other side, you'll know exactly how I felt when you walked out on me. Very desolate and very lost! See how you get on. Thank you for inviting me here, Daniel. (*She begins to rise, as if about to leave.*)

DANIEL: You're leaving? Please don't go!

PENELOPE: Daniel, can't you see there is nothing left for us.

DANIEL: I know I am completely to blame for everything that has gone wrong in our lives,but I'm willing to work at it and show you that I have changed dramatically, and there is nothing I wouldn't do for us. If you have any doubts then please share them with me.

PENELOPE: OK. Let's see then. How many times have you lied to me?

DANIEL: Em ... that is a difficult question.

PENELOPE: Why the hesitation? There always is an answer to a question. So tell me, how many times have you lied to me?

DANIEL: I lied to you mostly about my feelings. I was trying to cover up the truth so that you would not hate me.

PENELOPE: Was it worth it?

DANIEL: Yes and no.

PENELOPE: Whilst you were with me were you seeing anyone else?

DANIEL: No. I only ogled at Coral from time to time. We never did anything more than that. She knew that I liked her. And then you and I separated.

PENELOPE: You mean you left me?

DANIEL: Yes. I left you. I was wrong to do that.

PENELOPE: Did you know that two days after you left me I discovered I was pregnant?

DANIEL: Pregnant?

PENELOPE: Yes. I was actually six weeks pregnant. I knew I was feeling a little uneasy but I couldn't exactly work out why. Then came the dreadful news of you wanting to leave me and be a new man in America. My life was turned upside down. Without my family's continued support I would not have survived. I was a complete mess. Nobody knew about the baby, though. I kept that to myself. It wasn't something I could rejoice about, now was it?

DANIEL: What about the baby? How did you manage?

PENELOPE: I am very sorry to say that I had an abortion three days later. I would have loved to have had a child, but, without a father, how were things supposed to work? People would have labelled me as the disgraced woman with the burdened child. I couldn't have had that happen to me so I had to, sadly, have an abortion. It was mind-numbingly painful and unspeakably distressing. Had you not walked out of my life, we would have had a two-year-old today. Running around, talking, walking, laughing and calling us Mummy and Daddy. The baby would have loved us so much.

DANIEL: I am deeply ashamed and extremely sorry. But we tried so many times and nothing happened.

PENELOPE: Well it did. Obviously at the wrong time.

DANIEL: Why didn't you tell me?

PENELOPE: I didn't want you to come back just for the baby. That would have been so unfair. You would have left after a while anyway. Making matters far worse. If you were to have stayed for a particular reason then that should have been me. Fate saw you as an unfit father, so an innocent life had to come to an end. I certainly wasn't prepared to be a mother, given the circumstances. I was too depressed. I guess everything turned out for the best.

DANIEL: So I would have been a father if I had not left you? I can't believe it. I'm so sorry, my sweet.

PENELOPE: So you're a murderer, a womaniser, an egotist and a liar. And on the basis of your honesty you are expecting me to take you back?

DANIEL: I am not pleased with myself, but I would do anything for you. Penny, until you have lost something, you do not know how precious and significant it is. I regret so much. I was hoping you would recognise that. I have wasted my time being someone I am not.

PENELOPE: How much is a ticket to New York?

DANIEL: About three hundred pounds. Why do you ask?

PENELOPE: I will give you the three hundred pounds so that you can put yourself on the next available plane to New York and stay there!

DANIEL: All right then! I am so sorry to have taken up so much of your time, Penelope. I wish you all the best. Just to let you know I am absolutely heartbroken. I was looking forward to being with you again and starting a new family and basically enjoying and appreciating every minute that I am with you. I guess I am a lost cause. But thank you for listening to me and giving me a chance to explain myself.

PENELOPE: Before you disappear again, tell me, what do you really like about me?

DANIEL: Why are you making it worse? If I am not to be with you then I do not wish to think about you.

PENELOPE: You haven't answered my question.

DANIEL: (*Pause*)   I like your dazzling smile, your very beautiful eyes and I just cannot stop thinking how wonderful you look today. You still seem to remember my favourite colour. I love the way you talk. The way you laugh and make fun of me. I loved the way you used to squeeze my hand and then softly brush your cheek across mine and kiss me so gently that the kiss would linger even when you weren't there. I adored the way you would whisper something in my ear and I would have no idea what you had said because you were so quiet. And I loved being close to you. But that's all in the past now.

PENELOPE: Remember the night you proposed to me?

DANIEL: Yes. Vividly.

PENELOPE: Do you remember what you said?

DANIEL: Yes I do.

PENELOPE: Then why did you go to America and forget about me? I suppose it's my fault for trusting you so quickly. I should have waited a lot longer before saying yes.

DANIEL: I still have your wedding ring. It's in my pocket. I've kept it with me all the time. I didn't want to lose it. There were moments when I would wish you were still wearing it.

PENELOPE: Why don't you pawn it? Surely it's worth something?

DANIEL: I can see we're not getting anywhere. Penny, it was nice to see you again. I have enjoyed our meeting here today. I would love to see you again some time but now I must take my leave.

PENELOPE: So soon? I was going to delve in deeper and finally declare something extremely pleasing to your ears.

DANIEL: Such as?

PENELOPE: Daniel Sullivan, the truth is that I did read your letter many times. Each time I read it I found a different meaning. There were so many hidden connotations in your profound verse that led me to believe that you were very serious about us. It made me think very hard about my future with you. As an impecunious man you have come to my door. As a dejected man you are seeking my friendship and love, and as a disloyal husband you are asking for forgiveness. I find myself at the end of a long and winding road. So what should I do?

DANIEL: I thought you had a field day with my letter.

PENELOPE: Oh no! That was all talk. I just wanted to see your reaction. That letter was absolutely private. I'm not that callous.

DANIEL: You must understand that I didn't hide anything from you.

PENELOPE: Do you know what you are asking me to do? You are asking me to forget about the past and begin a new life. Now the question is, is that feasible?

DANIEL: Well, I think it is.

PENELOPE: Daniel I have never laid eyes on another man since I met you. I find you very charming and, oh, you are still so handsome that I cannot take my eyes off you. I have also come to realise how much I have really missed you. To be honest, for the past few minutes I have been looking at you quite differently. (*Pause*) What are you doing tonight?

DANIEL: Nothing. Why?

PENELOPE: Good. I was hoping to hear that. I was thinking maybe we should catch up on a few things.

DANIEL: Where would you like to meet?

PENELOPE: My cottage.

DANIEL: What time?

PENELOPE: Think of a time and then turn up. Let's see if you still have the gift.

DANIEL: All right. I'll see you when you're ready. Would you like me to bring anything?

PENELOPE: Do you still suffer from back pain?

DANIEL: Not so much.

PENELOPE: You may need your hot-water bottle.

DANIEL: What about your father?

PENELOPE: Don't worry, he'll know nothing about it until I say something.

DANIEL: Penny, you must talk to your father first. He's going to kill me if he finds out about this.

PENELOPE: You just concentrate on making me a happy woman and I'll take care of the rest. I can handle my father.

DANIEL: Are you sure?

PENELOPE: I know what I am doing. Please? Trust me?
DANIEL: When is the next Dex?
PENELOPE: It's coming up in a few weeks. Would you like to attend the Dex?
DANIEL: Your father's going to nail me to the ground and skin me alive!
PENELOPE: Remember, I'll be there to protect you. I won't put your name on the guest list. I'll give you an exact time to arrive and I'll secretly let you in.
DANIEL: You seem to have it all worked out.
PENELOPE: Daniel, I'm really hoping that everything will work out between us. I am giving you a second chance so that you can prove to me that you are definitely a changed man. If you disappoint me again...
DANIEL: Let's not ruin the ambience by thinking about the negative side. I promise to prove to you that I am a changed man. I love you, Penelope Devereux. I have missed you very much. I cannot wait to be with you, my sweetheart.
PENELOPE: I'd better run along. Max will be driving round soon. I'll see you later. The roses might come in handy for this evening, with a bottle of wine.
DANIEL: I understand.

As PENELOPE *is about to rise* DANIEL *grabs her hand, leans forward and softly kisses her.* PENELOPE *becomes shy and smiles. Then she leaves his side.* DANIEL *watches her exit.*

SCENE TWELVE

The cook is due to meet with her employer, FREDERICK DEVEREUX, *to discuss something important. As usual she is made to wait. Whilst she is seated near* FREDERICK*'s desk,* PENCHARD *is watching her. There are no exchanges or any kind of gestures. Just awkward silence for* ROSE. *After a little while* FREDERICK *emerges. He walks to his desk and begins to look at some paperwork. He does not acknowledge* ROSE *immediately. Finally* FREDERICK *decides to address her. By now* ROSE *is quite nervous.*

FREDERICK: I am cut short for time, Rose. I would like you to be very quick, especially as you are on duty. I do not like my staff wasting time when I am paying them.
ROSE: Yes, Mr Devereux.
PENCHARD: She insisted that she speak with you at once.
FREDERICK: Please explain yourself.
ROSE: I need to have some holiday.
FREDERICK: Need? That is quite an impertinent word, isn't it, Rose? Holidays are for people who crack under pressure. Some people need free time to understand their lives better, experience laziness and satisfy a preventable desire. However, some of us do not. So you are demanding a holiday? When?
ROSE: From Monday the 12th onwards until Friday.
FREDERICK: Five whole days? A week before the Dex? Rose, you are mocking my rules. You are standing before me requesting what I have decreed in the past as an unsuitable period to even consider for time off. The very plain answer is 'no'.

ROSE: Mr Devereux, I perfectly understand and respect and admire your rulings, but on this occasion I am sincerely apologetic to have to go against those terms. My husband is in hospital. He is due to have quite a complicated operation and I need to be with him.

FREDERICK: Your tone, your manner of speaking and your unnecessary use of the word 'need' shock me. Your husband does not need you beside him. That is your emotional flaw. You believe that because of your relationship or, should I say, as duty bounds. But the fact of the matter is you have a choice. My choice is that you stay until the Dex is over. I require every member of staff's cooperation and personal effort to ensure that everything runs very smoothly. Your absence will trigger an unfavourable discussion amongst the rest of the mansion staff. The discussion being, why are they not able to do the same thing. I cannot allow that to happen.

ROSE: I'm sorry, Mr Devereux, but I have to be with my husband in his hour of need.

FREDERICK: Am I correct in saying that you have a nineteen-year-old daughter at home who is already looking after him?

ROSE: Yes.

FREDERICK: Am I correct in saying that she is currently a lady of leisure?

ROSE: Yes.

FREDERICK: Then I have solved your problem.

ROSE: Pardon?

FREDERICK: Surely your daughter can become the indispensable nurse by his ailing bedside?

ROSE: It's not quite the same.

FREDERICK: If you ask me again regarding this subject then I will personally suspend you until further notice. In the meantime I am resolved to deduct your salary by a small percentage purely because of your foolishness and audacity in requesting the impossible and wasting my precious time.

ROSE: Mr Devereux, that is not fair. I did the right thing by coming to you and discussing the matter openly.

FREDERICK: Am I wrong to trust you?

ROSE: No.

FREDERICK: Rose, the Dex is always overall a success and I wish to keep it that way. And now your sudden urge to be absent is signalling disloyalty, defiance and aggression. I do not wish to witness this sort of attitude from a respectable lady like yourself.

ROSE: This isn't my fault. Mr Devereux, please help me out.

FREDERICK: Rose, is there anything else that you need to discuss?

ROSE: Apart from this matter, no.

FREDERICK: And as a faithful employee, you are being truthful?

ROSE: Of course!

FREDERICK: So why are you lying to me?

ROSE: I'm sorry?

FREDERICK: You are quite the sly fox. What a believable act! I commend you. Sadly, this sort of pretence has dug you a very deep hole.

ROSE: How do you mean?

FREDERICK: There is no operation, is there, Rose? There is actually nothing to worry about. You are wanting to take time off so that you can search for your younger daughter, who has chosen to run away with the village scoundrel. Have I struck the right chord?

ROSE: Well...

FREDERICK: Your enormous effort is actually not for a complicated operation for your dearest husband but a quest to seek out your ill-disciplined daughter, Sarah. She has once again decided to run away with the notorious village rogue. You and your husband disagreed with her getting married.

ROSE: Where did you get all this information from?

FREDERICK: If I am correct please state your affirmation.

ROSE: Mr Devereux, I wish to keep my private life private.
FREDERICK: What you need for children these days are very tight leashes. It's all very well coming out to work, but at the same time you must instil some sort of discipline. Especially where young girls are concerned. Girls have the strength to bring you down quicker than the boys do. The frivolous girls have a lot more to lose than the young lads. We are talking distinct levels of pride.
ROSE: Mr Devereux, I would be very grateful if you were able to grant me this period of time off.
FREDERICK: Parents have children under the belief that they strive to be good role models. As they grow up they see and understand what their parents are like. They will learn to mimic your mannerisms and shall gain knowledge of how you perceive the outside world. Now, if you let them do whatever they want, and I literally mean that, then you are simply preparing yourself to be persecuted at their hands. Furthermore, you lose all control over them and become the one who has to pick up the pieces when everything goes wrong. You become their most committed doormat. You may think you are being strong and didactic but at the end of the day they successfully wrap you around their little finger. Your daughter is making a complete fool of you and instead of punishing and disciplining her, here you are lying to me. At your position's expense. You do not know how to be dogmatic. You are a very poor and laughable example as a parent. Am I correct to say that this is the third time she has run away?
ROSE: Yes.
FREDERICK: So why does she still have her freedom? Why has she the liberty to make choices? Why can you not lock her up in a room and throw away the key?
ROSE: It's extremely difficult...
FREDERICK: 'Extremely difficult', she says! I thought she was your daughter? I thought she was your responsibility? You

gave her life. You call the shots. Not her. And I must say, her choice of partner sickens me. Billy Higgins, or should I use his infamous gang name? Bigs. What on earth does your husband do? If a father is unable to give anything to his offspring the least he can do is give them all good manners. It does not tax the brain too much and it certainly does not cost any money. I suppose he just twiddles his thumbs and relaxes all day until you, the dedicated slave, arrive home to prepare the dinner. Then his challenge is no doubt how to eat like a pig?!

ROSE: Mr Devereux!

FREDERICK: The truth has a murderous head and the truth can hurt a lot of people. You were determined to shadow the ugly truth because you felt the need to protect your dreadful and corrupted family. You're very brave, Rose, but also very stupid. You should recall that you, as my employee, have no choice about telling the truth. You say it plainly and you say it without any embellishment. Are you clear about that?

ROSE: Yes. Of course.

FREDERICK: Rose, did someone put you up to this?

ROSE: No. Absolutely not. I came here of my own accord.

FREDERICK: You have come to me with a painstaking matter and I, being the ultimate arbiter have laid down the law. If you kindly comply with this directive, our paths will not cross again. Penchard, please could you show Rose the way out.

ROSE: But, Mr Devereux, I thought that having been your sincere and longest-serving employee you would at your total discretion loosen the terms a little bit.

FREDERICK: Why on earth would you think that, Rose? I don't see the necessity to do so. You are all to be treated the same way. I cannot have one rule for you and another for the other members. That would lead to utter chaos within the working ranks.

ROSE: In that case, as of today I am giving you my six weeks' notice.

FREDERICK: You are very welcome to put it in writing and I will simply dispose of it. There are no grounds for your resignation. There is nothing wrong. You are just being small-minded and recalcitrant, as many women are. Thank you for coming and highlighting your concerns. That will be all.
ROSE: With all due respect, Mr Devereux, I was hoping for a little bit of compassion.
FREDERICK: What are you, Rose? Nothing but a mere employee. You are the mansion's cook. That is all. Why do you feel that you are seen as a unique member of staff? Is there something that I have not noted about you that leads you to this definition? Are you rich?
ROSE: I wish I was.
FREDERICK: You are here to obey my orders and make absolutely certain that all culinary requirements are met. In return I pay you your living. A very simple and comprehensible equation.
ROSE: You have such a remarkable way with words.
FREDERICK: You will find yourself a few pounds short at the end of this month.
ROSE: Mr Devereux, please?
FREDERICK: Get out before I summon security to drag you out.
ROSE: I thought you were someone who would understand.
FREDERICK: I understand that I no longer need to speak with you. You have wasted my time. Next time I will not be as kind. Now please leave. Or I will dismiss you.
ROSE: (*very distraught*) That's not fair.
FREDERICK: Unsurprisingly, life is not fair.
ROSE: I am so sorry to have troubled you, Mr Devereux.

ROSE, *sadly, leaves her seat.* PENCHARD *also jumps out of his seat and quickly rushes to her side in order to escort her out of the room.* ROSE *hangs her head with great misery. She walks out slowly.*

SCENE THIRTEEN

PENELOPE DEVEREUX *arrives home very late. As she creeps in, her father notices her cautious entry. He watches her closely, then he breaks the silence.*

FREDERICK: Is Daniel in town for long?
PENELOPE: (*startled*) Father!
FREDERICK: Well is he?
PENELOPE: (*very slowly*) I . . . I do hope so.
FREDERICK: Does your education mean anything to you?
PENELOPE: I was going to tell you.
FREDERICK: You grow up, you go to school, you learn, you understand and then you start to build.
PENELOPE: I really was.
FREDERICK: You build this unique picture of your life and you say to yourself 'Is this what I want?' 'Is this good for me?' 'Does this have my best interests at heart?'
PENELOPE: But I love him. I have always loved him.
FREDERICK: Oh, you are a dim girl. I didn't know we had such stupidity running in the family! Love! Love! Love has nothing to offer. People who dream fall in love. Real people appreciate emotional capacity. Love makes you severely blind and mentally it cripples you so that your understanding and common sense are totally distorted.
PENELOPE: I can't help the way I feel.
FREDERICK: Would you like him to suffer?
PENELOPE: Please no. No. You must not.
FREDERICK: I'm sure Nancy has been through the inescapable consequences with you many times.
PENELOPE: Did she tell you about this? She promised she wouldn't.

FREDERICK: She has more sense than you and luckily she disapproves.

PENELOPE: She promised.

FREDERICK: Women are so weak and vulnerable. Why you girls cannot control your emotions I'll never know.

PENELOPE: Daniel isn't a bad person, Father!

FREDERICK: And to think you went behind my back! You went against my wishes. How dare you, Penelope! How dare you!

PENELOPE: Father, please? You must understand.

FREDERICK: This is exactly the reason why women, many years ago, were seen as useful tools only within the home. Women were meant to be uneducated. They were perceived as being with only culinary and maternal skills. Beyond that, women would create far too many complications and ruin society as a whole. They simply do not hold sensible thoughts and their loose acceptance of meagre standards renders them desperate and bemused. Men were always the breadwinners, the proper decision makers and the ones that knew best, and as time has progressed men still are the breadwinners, the proper decision makers and the glorious ones who certainly know best. Over the years, we have heard countless charges of injustice towards women, imposition of an inferiority complex and above all that women have been subject to harassment within the home and within the working environment. Why do you think that happened, Penelope? Why?

PENELOPE: (*becoming tense*) I don't know why.

FREDERICK: (*becoming fierce*) Because women have this unmatched ability for making mistakes and for drawing attention to their needy state. You are seen as dependants and you still lack the gift of a decent and healthy education. You never learn. You keep slipping up. Don't you, Miss Penelope Elizabeth Devereux?

PENELOPE: I am only able to look at Daniel with loving eyes.

I could never detest him. Believe me, I have tried, Father. I really did want to hate him for what he had done to me, but, when I truly questioned my feelings, they became feelings of affection and sympathy.

FREDERICK: You have just proved my point. I can only applaud your belief in my theory.

PENELOPE: I want to start again. I'm sure everything will be different.

FREDERICK: If you continue to see him, I will lock you in your room and never allow you to set foot outside this mansion. I do not appreciate disorderly manners from anyone. If you have to be punished then you will be punished. As you would expect, before punishing you I would need to punish the unrelenting and hard-hearted Daniel Sullivan.

PENELOPE: You can punish me if you wish, Father, but please could you give him one more chance? That is all I ask of you. Just one more chance.

FREDERICK: Very well, then. You have decided to play this by your rules. So you choose, his heart or his guts or his brain?

PENELOPE: I do not want to lose him, Father. I beg you.

FREDERICK: You have lost him, Penelope, my dear.

PENELOPE: You may say all you want, Father, but I just cannot let go of him. Why are you so set on making me unhappy?

FREDERICK: I am not the one to blame here! Your acid tongue and stubborn nature are only preparing you for your biggest downfall.

PENELOPE: Daniel really cares about me.

FREDERICK: And I care about you. Daniel's sole purpose is to use you and dump you like a pile of rubbish.

PENELOPE: I am not convinced. He's changed so much.

FREDERICK: Penchard will be watching your every move. You have been warned.

PENELOPE *begins to cry.*

FREDERICK: Your tears are tears of idiocy. I shall not yield. Penelope, my child, you know my methods of edict. You have learnt to grow up with them very well. To emphasise them so strongly and to execute them without fail surely indicates that I have no desire to reverse them. And here you are trying to manipulate the course of inevitability. Now, go to bed and calm yourself. I will see you in the morning and please do not plan anything sinister. Penelope, dear, you are one of my angels. I will always have your best interests at heart.

PENELOPE *exits miserably.*

SCENE FOURTEEN

PATRICK *and* CORAL *are taking a break in the kitchen. They are sitting at a small round table, having tea and biscuits.*

CORAL: Any news?
PATRICK: No, nothing promising. Everyone I go to has no answers for me. They dismiss my queries very quickly.
CORAL: It's called the evil blight of the Devereux sting. There certainly is information out there, but nobody will cooperate for fear of being punished by Devereux himself. I tell you, he is one brutal and vindictive monster! Only a terrible disease will wear him down, nothing else.
PATRICK: I wish I knew the truth. I wish I could be sure that he was definitely responsible for her disappearance.
CORAL: There may be another way.
PATRICK: What else could I possibly do?
CORAL: Penchard. Have you thought about making friends with him?
PATRICK: I'm just a gardener. Why would he want to know me?
CORAL: True. Penchard is very pompous and arrogant, but he does have a mind full of information. Remember, he is Devereux's sidekick so he would know absolutely everything.
PATRICK: So do you think he'd know about Michelle?
CORAL: If you tell him how wonderful he is and flatter him, I am sure he will start to open up. And gradually you will get the information you need.
PATRICK: Your plan seems like a good idea, but he always turns his nose up at me. He'll never have a personal conversation with me.

MEESHA *enters with a bucket of wet clothes. She drops the bucket down hard.*

MEESHA: I shouldn't have washed those gowns. I've ruined them now.
CORAL: Why did you need to wash them in the first place?
MEESHA: All due respect to Veronica Devereux, but I can't wear what one of them has worn. It feels a little disgusting. So I thought by washing them I would get a fresh new look. Unfortunately, the fabric has reacted badly to the washing powder. I think some of the colours have clashed as well.
PATRICK: They must be expensive.
MEESHA: Naturally! I would not settle for anything less! Any more tea in the pot?
CORAL: Yes, I think so.

MEESHA *pours herself a cup of tea and joins them both.*

PATRICK: My patience is fast running out.
CORAL: I'm telling you, Penchard is the one who will give you that inside information.
MEESHA: What are we talking about?
PATRICK: My ongoing dilemma.
CORAL: If Patrick can get close to Penchard then he might be able to get some answers.
PATRICK: Question is how?
MEESHA: I haven't seen Jim or Raisor for a while now. I wonder if they would have any leads.
PATRICK: No. I asked them. (*sighing*) I feel so desperate. She can't just disappear into thin air.
CORAL: Penchard is your best bet. It's just a case of squeezing the details out of him.
MEESHA: (*To* CORAL) Actually, why don't you do the squeezing for him?
CORAL: How do you mean?

MEESHA: Well, we all know how Penchard enjoys female company. Wear a buttoned see-through top and pout your lips and you will be golden. He will begin to tell you things that under ordinary circumstances he would not.
PATRICK: That's an excellent idea!
MEESHA: Go on, Coral, you know you have got what it takes to spin him around. Oh and guess what, I already have a buttoned top in my locker.
CORAL: I can't do it now.
PATRICK: What's stopping you? I'd really appreciate it if you were to do this for me. Please?
CORAL: It's just that...
MEESHA: Shall I go and call him? He's in his den.
PATRICK: Coral, please? I will be ever so grateful.
CORAL: I suppose.

Suddenly we hear quick footsteps coming towards the kitchen.

MEESHA: Sounds like Penchard clomping his heels. Quickly, go to my locker and put on that blouse. Hurry! Hurry!
CORAL: But I'm not ready yet!
MEESHA: Patrick and I will hide whilst you work your magic. Go on. Stop looking like a lemon and get a move on. Now is the perfect time.
CORAL: Oh, all right! You both owe me big time.

MEESHA *and* PATRICK *hide behind a tall column and peer over.* CORAL *disappears for a few seconds and reappears wearing a pink frilly blouse. It seems a little tight for her.*

PATRICK: I really do hope this is going to work.
MEESHA: Coral is a pro. Don't worry. There is a reason why we get free salmon from sleazy Sebastian.

PENCHARD *emerges with quite a serious expression. He stops to take a good look around the kitchen and then moves towards the round table.*

PATRICK: Are you sure he can't see us from there?
MEESHA: Will you stop fretting! We're absolutely fine.
PATRICK: You're stepping on my toes!
MEESHA: I'm sorry! Could you move over a little bit?
PATRICK: What if we get caught?
MEESHA: Shut up! Coral, get on with it!
PATRICK: I really hope you know what you are doing!
PENCHARD: Is anyone here? Where the devil are you all?
CORAL: (*sticking her bust out and pouting her lips*) Sorry, Penchard, were you after me? I didn't hear you come in.
PENCHARD: (*He gives her an odd look.*) I require all the menus from Tuesday until Friday. Do you have those?
CORAL: Yes, I do have them somewhere but even before we go into all that, Penchard, I have been meaning to tell you something. It's just that with pressures from work, it hasn't been possible. (*She begins to draw closer to him*).
MEESHA: Here we go. Don't even blink, Pat, you might miss something.
PENCHARD: I am really cut short for time. Do you have the menus or not?
CORAL: Every time I see you, the way you walk, the way you look and the way your bald patch glistens under the evening stars, I get this tingling feeling right here. (*She points to her chest.*) Do you want to see? (*She takes his hand and puts it on her chest.*)
PENCHARD: (*a little startled*) What are you doing?
CORAL: Because you're standing before me in such a dashing and irresistible manner, my heart has become restless. Can you feel the rhythm?
PENCHARD: (*beginning to blush*) I . . . I was hoping to see the (*His tone softens.*) . . . menus.

CORAL: Boom... boom... boom... boom. Do you see what kind of effect you have on me? (*She starts to breathe heavily.*)
PENCHARD: I had no idea.
CORAL: You're always too busy to even notice me. Whereas I have been yearning for a magical moment with you.
MEESHA & PATRICK: Yuck!
PENCHARD: What was that noise?
CORAL: (*She moves her face directly in front of his.*) When I look at you, your eyes and tantalising bald patch, I just feel like grabbing you like this. (*She grabs both his arms.*) And just feeling your unnerving warmth from your luscious lips, your sweet tender look and much more.
PENCHARD: I must say, you are very beautiful. Your bosom holds much warmth. I always thought that you hated me.
CORAL: Never! If I have ever come across too strong, it's only because I thought I couldn't have you beside me.
PENCHARD: I'm so glad that you like me. I have always fantasised about you.
MEESHA: (*whispering*) Perve!
PENCHARD: There were many moments when you would appear before me with your full breasts and glorious face and I would stare and think to myself 'My goodness me, you are every bit the woman I have dreamt of.' Don't take me wrong, naturally I comprehend that it's not just what's on the outside, it is what's underneath that counts.
CORAL: Oh Penchard, hold me close. (*Whispering under her breath*) You bloody fool!
PATRICK: How awful! This is too hard to watch.
MEESHA: Don't you dare close your eyes! We're now getting to the juicier part.
CORAL: Penchard, stop wasting time. Every moment with you is precious.

They hug uncomfortably. PENCHARD *holds on more than* CORAL. MEESHA *and* PATRICK *burst out laughing.* PENCHARD *stops.*

PENCHARD: What was that?
CORAL: It's my wailing heart. It wants you so badly. Don't go.
PENCHARD: I swear I heard human laughter.
CORAL: Your ears are deceiving you, Penchard ... my sweet. Oh, the buttons on this blouse are really scratching my skin. Maybe I should undo a few of them. (*Her cleavage appears.*)
PENCHARD: (*He gazes at them.*)   I really wish it were my night off so I could hold you gently, smell your delicate hair and amorously fondle your beauty.
PATRICK: I think I'm going to be sick!
CORAL: Well, why don't we make the most of this moment now, Penchard? Why can't we just pretend that your time off is right now?
PENCHARD: You are truly brave my darling! (*He is about to kiss and hold her hard.*)
MEESHA: He is such a slimy beast!
CORAL: No, wait. What if someone walks in?
PENCHARD: We will pretend nothing happened and go our own ways.
CORAL: Penchard, before I can wholly give myself to you, I need to know one thing.
PENCHARD: What is that, my lovely?
CORAL: People are accusing you of being involved in ... no, I can't say it! (*Pretending to become distressed.*)
PENCHARD: Oh please, my darling. Share your concern with me. I will protect you, always. I do not want to see your infatuation fade away because of your anxiety.
CORAL: Are you sure you want to know?
PENCHARD: I am already blinded by your passion for me. Of course I will understand.
CORAL: Certain people are claiming that you had something to do with that girl's disappearance.
PENCHARD: What girl?
CORAL: You know, the one linked with Benjamin Devereux.

PENCHARD: (*becoming serious*)   What are you getting at, Coral?
CORAL: Don't move away from me. My bosom feels lonely without your warmth.
PENCHARD: What have you heard?
CORAL: Is she dead ... my darling Penchard?
PENCHARD: Do we have to discuss this? It is getting in the way of our affection towards each other.
CORAL: I must know because (*pretending to get upset*) ... I hate it when they call you a murderer!
PENCHARD: Really? Is that what people are saying?
CORAL: It truly breaks my heart! I have these sincere feelings for you and there they are, accusing you of these horrid things!
PENCHARD: The truth is I had nothing to do with her death.
CORAL: (*shocked*)   So she's actually dead?
PENCHARD: Yes. She died the same day. Her body's safely tucked away, though.
CORAL: Really?
PENCHARD: Now, enough of all this nonsense. Let us carry on with what nature intended.
CORAL: I can't, Penchard. You have to reassure me genuinely that you had no hand in killing her. I want to be able to trust you completely. How can we possibly begin a fruitful relationship if we cannot be honest with each other? There is nothing I wouldn't do for you.
PENCHARD: All right. The girl we are talking about died accidentally. She was not supposed to die. The boys made a grave mistake.
CORAL: The boys?
PENCHARD: Mr Devereux wanted to scare her off a little bit. Instead the boys went too far.
CORAL: Oh I see!
PATRICK: I can't believe it! It's really her, then?
MEESHA: What evil monsters!

PENCHARD: Coral, darling, just look into my eyes. What do you see?
CORAL: Fear?
PENCHARD: Love. Lust. Attraction. The joining of two dear souls. I want you, Coral. I really want you. Never have I had such powerful feelings for a woman! You bring great joy to my heart.
CORAL: So what is happening now?
PENCHARD: That case is closed now. We have other things to deal with. We are far too busy with more important issues.
CORAL: Did you know her name?
PENCHARD: What is it with all these questions? You're simply ruining the moment.
CORAL: I just hate looking at you with distressed eyes. I only want to look at you with love and admiration. You mean a lot to me ... your body, too.
PENCHARD: Her name was ... let me think ... Michelle. Yes, that's it, Michelle.
PATRICK: My poor sister! My poor baby sister! Why did they do it? Why?
PENCHARD: Coral, it is necessary that I depart now. Before I go please send me off with a nourishing and very ardent kiss. So passionate that I can truly feel your moist lips.
CORAL: Oh no! I have an awful headache! It's really throbbing, right here!
PENCHARD: So now you're saying I do not mean anything to you?
CORAL: When I have one of these headaches I find it hard to concentrate. I would be lying if I said I could go all the way with our passion now.
PENCHARD: You enthral me, Coral. You are so honest and I am so rude. I should respect you for being honest. Let's set a secret rendezvous. Just you and me. Under the stars, in the fresh fields, totally naked!
CORAL: It sounds very encouraging.

PENCHARD: How about next Wednesday? I'm free all day. I could pack a small picnic and a very velvety sheet for extra comfort.
CORAL: I will have to let you know.
PENCHARD: Shall I take that as a 'yes'?
CORAL: Eh? Why not? I will love to see you naked.
PENCHARD: Farewell, my sweet. Next Wednesday you shall see me with more skin tone and debonair contours. I also am a firm believer in 'big is beautiful.' I am certain that you will see me in a different light and equally you shall be very impressed. I aim to please and I miss your bosom already.
CORAL: Goodbye, Penchard. I am already counting the hours. You lucky devil!

As PENCHARD *exits,* PATRICK *and* MEESHA *come out.*

PATRICK: The bastard has destroyed my life. I'm going to kill him.
MEESHA: Are you all right, Coral?
CORAL: I think a long hot bath with bleach is in order. He has such bad breath. He is absolutely revolting!
MEESHA: At least you have an adventurous date for next Wednesday! Think of all that lovely murky skin! By the way, you can keep that blouse!

CORAL *gives her an infuriated look.*

SCENE FIFTEEN

A young, slightly unkempt journalist appears armed with a camera round his neck, clipboard and pen. After being quizzed by PENCHARD, *he becomes rather fidgety and apprehensive.* JACK HADDY, *tall, slim and with quite a rigorous manner, enters the room. He is the organiser of the Dex, an occasion which is always publicised.*

JACK: You seem too young for this job. What is your name?
SAMUEL: Samuel Calcott, sir.
JACK: Mr Calcott, do you honestly expect me to take you seriously? How am I supposed to trust your abilities when you do not even know how to hold your pen straight?
SAMUEL: I do have experience.
JACK: You mean you lack experience. You have perspiration on your brow.
SAMUEL: I have covered other events before.
JACK: Intrigue me.
SAMUEL: The Fezaria-Aston Brinkster and Vales charity event and the Fezaria-Aston Business Acquisition conference.
JACK: Only two events under your belt and the editor has sent you to cover the most prestigious event of the year? My goodness me! What is happening to the world these days? Only two nugatory events and now you seem ready for the sacred Dex. How presumptuous! Whatever happened to the skilful Simon Thresnell? He was the best.
SAMUEL: He was promoted.
JACK: Exactly my point. Of course and why shouldn't he be? His appearance was delightfully smart, his demeanour always amiable and his journalistic skills boasted many

years of impressive experience covering opulent events. You are nothing compared to him.
PENCHARD: Yes. Absolutely nothing.
SAMUEL: I will do my best.
JACK: Your weak tone even reeks of your inability to cope with journalism.
PENCHARD: (*shaking his head*)   Inability to cope!
SAMUEL: Mr Sarring will be very angry if I do not carry out my duties here. He did say he has confidence in me.
JACK: (*sarcastically*)   Well then, I am reassured!
PENCHARD: Dreadful, really dreadful!
SAMUEL: I was thinking we should not only do a feature regarding the event, which is normally the case, but also a showcase of the people and family behind the Devereux Extravaganza.
JACK: Explain your thoughts, please.
SAMUEL: Well, each year, the Dex vaunts powerful, wealthy figures, vast business opportunities and immense changes within the business and financial worlds, On this particular occasion I was thinking of doing exactly the same, but also another spectacular feature about the august and benevolent dynasty behind it. What do you think?
JACK: I actually believe that to be quite a daring but magnificent idea! What a divine combination you have envisaged. I'm glad I never doubted your capabilities. You certainly fit the cap, young man.
PENCHARD: Daring and magnificent, young man!
JACK: So proceed further. What else does this impressive piece demand?
SAMUEL: I would be grateful if I could speak with one or two prominent members of the family. Namely, Ms Sophie Devereux and Master Thomas Devereux?
PENCHARD: They are not available to speak to.
JACK: Now, hold your horses, Penchard. Ms Sophie Devereux may be interested, but Master Thomas Devereux we shall exclude. Ms Devereux likes a little bit of publicity.

SAMUEL: What about Master Benjamin Devereux?
JACK: Let's just stick to one gracious and distinguished figure. Penchard, please ask Ms Devereux kindly. (*Scribbling a small note*) and could you give her this note. Thank you.

PENCHARD *exits.*

JACK: Any slanderous and obscene talk and I shall throw you out of this mansion. Is that clear?
SAMUEL: I will be fair. (*Pause*) So do you organise the grand Dex each year?
JACK: You do not have to fill these silences. Please keep your nose close to your pen.
SAMUEL: OK. Could I ask how long you're allowing for the interview?
JACK: As little time as possible. We are all very busy people.
SAMUEL: You must have a huge amount of responsibility. I mean, this is the Dex. Everybody talks about it. Everybody wants to be invited to the Dex. You must be so proud to be the chief organiser?

JACK *remains silent. He gives* SAMUEL *an irritated look.*

SAMUEL: The mansion is of such superior quality. It is absolutely incredible. I have never seen such brilliance in architecture. It must take hundreds and thousands to maintain such grandeur. I certainly will remember my visit here. This splendid mansion would make any soul thoroughly jealous. I would love to spend the entire day here. I wonder how much this sort of property costs. Millions and millions, I suspect.

PENCHARD *returns with* SOPHIE.

JACK: (*He stands up.*) Ah, Ms Devereux, thank you for coming at such short notice. Please do take a seat. This is the journalist from the *Royal Fezaria-Aston Journal*. What is your name again?

SAMUEL: (*He rises.*)   Samuel Calcott, nice to meet you. (*He extends his hand.*)

PENCHARD: She does not shake hands with journalists.

SOPHIE: (*She sits down.*)   Begin!

JACK: Now, Mr Calcott, please remember what I said.

SAMUEL: Yes, of course. It is absolutely wonderful to have this opportunity to speak with you. My first question to you is how do you feel at this time of year? The run up to the Dex must be exciting.

SOPHIE: Yes it is. I look forward to it each year.

SAMUEL: Do you feel very special to be a part of it?

SOPHIE: Naturally.

SAMUEL: The cordial invitations state the names of very powerful and wealthy guests. If the name Christopher Marsh appeared, how would you feel?

SOPHIE: I beg your pardon?

SAMUEL: The name Christopher Marsh. Does it ring any bells with you Ms Devereux?

SOPHIE: That name has exhausted and impaired me. I do not wish to discuss this any further.

JACK: Mr Calcott! Please keep your questions in line!

SAMUEL: Yes, of course. If this obscure individual were to accompany one of the guests to the Dex, what would your reaction be?

JACK: Who on earth is this Christopher Marsh?

PENCHARD: Christopher Marsh?

SAMUEL: Someone of great significance. Hence my questions concerning him. He is responsible for altering a major part of the dynasty, is he not?

SOPHIE: I want you to leave, Mr Calcott.

JACK: Mr Calcott, you have thoroughly disappointed Ms Devereux and myself. I have to summon security now.

SAMUEL: His offspring must be in their twenties now. Are they coming to the Dex as well?
JACK: Penchard, please call security.
SOPHIE: Your interviewing skills are in rather poor taste. Please tell your editor he is to see us straight after the Dex is over. I am quite sure he will appreciate an early retirement.
SAMUEL: I was only asking questions that were prepared for me. None of these are my own. Do you miss Christopher Marsh? He must have been your knight in shining armour.
JACK: Please refrain from any further questions, young man. You have said quite enough.
SAMUEL: It also says here that due to your longstanding grief you have chosen to remain a spinster and faithful to Christopher Marsh, and you have not had the privilege of raising children.
SOPHIE: How dare you! How dare you come into this mansion and insult me and poke fun at my past!
SAMUEL: I was only sent to do a job, madam. I was not aware that these questions would be derogatory.
SOPHIE: You are a journalist. Journalists have a great skill in manipulating the truth. Another name for a journalist is sycophant.

Suddenly security rushes in and takes MR CALCOTT *away.*

SOPHIE: Next time, Mr Haddy, please use your head and not your ego.
JACK: I apologise for the utter inconvenience.
SOPHIE: You are not here to fuel awkward embarrassment, you are not here to cause grating drama and you are certainly not here to revitalise any past history. You are here as your contract suggests. I recommend that you read it again. I am sure you need reminding of your status. You have definitely forgotten ours.

JACK: I am very humiliated. I am profoundly repentant. Please forgive me.

SOPHIE *exits angrily.*

SCENE SIXTEEN

BENJAMIN *is consoling his upset Aunt. They are in her study.*

BENJAMIN: Auntie Sophie, you must tell me. What is the matter? I have never seen you like this. What on earth happened?
SOPHIE: The whole world moves on but I can't. People fall in love but I have no love. People achieve many things in their life but I seem to have no life.
BENJAMIN: What has brought this on all of a sudden?
SOPHIE: A stupid and ignorant journalist. He was asking very rude and offensive questions.
BENJAMIN: What did he say exactly?
SOPHIE: He used the name Christopher Marsh many times. He was asking me about him.
BENJAMIN: Oh!
SOPHIE: I miss him.
BENJAMIN: The villagers have spoken about Christopher Marsh and I must admit I have stood there and listened attentively.
SOPHIE: What did they say?
BENJAMIN: You don't want to know.
SOPHIE: Yes I do. What have they been saying?
BENJAMIN: Auntie Sophie, this really is not a good topic to go into.
SOPHIE: Well?
BENJAMIN: Most of them say that you are responsible for his death. Pardon me for saying this, but you also had an intimate relationship with him and then chose to abandon him. In the end you ordered that he should suffer a painful

death and his progeny should be either killed or given away to low-class citizens because that is what he was.

SOPHIE: (*starting to sob*)   That's not fair. That's so evil.

BENJAMIN: It is all in the grapevine. Nobody seems to know the truth.

SOPHIE: Except for me.

BENJAMIN: You should put them right, Auntie Sophie.

SOPHIE: (*calming down a little bit*)   What is the point? Even if the truth were known, people would still disparage and curse me.

BENJAMIN: I must say, I have always wondered about you and this Christopher Marsh.

SOPHIE: Because of him, I have never married. You know the little cove next to my bedroom? That is full of memorabilia of Christopher Marsh and his son.

BENJAMIN: (*stunned*)   So you actually have a son?

SOPHIE: Yes, I have a son.

BENJAMIN: Where is he? What is he doing now? Why isn't he with you?

SOPHIE: Benjamin you must swear on your life that you will never repeat what I am about to tell you. You swear?

BENJAMIN: Absolutely! You can confide in me, Auntie Sophie. I will respect your wishes.

SOPHIE: I was a little younger than you. He used to drive a tractor on Mr Warrington's farm. Next to the farm there were so many pretty flowerbeds. They had such colourful flowers that I just had to go and pick them and bring them home. First time I met Christopher, he shouted at me and said 'Get off this property. You are trespassing. You will get into trouble.' I wish I had listened. As I was young and rebellious from time to time, his warning fell on deaf ears. I continued to visit the flowerbeds until one day Christopher jumped off his tractor and we came face to face. Again he echoed the same thing. I looked straight at him and smiled and gave him a red rose. It obviously didn't mean anything. I just wanted him to stop shouting at me. He was very handsome and well built. I remember his shirt was a little torn at the side. I asked why he was wearing a torn shirt. He explained that the shirt was his best garment yet. I felt a little sorry for him and I said 'Don't worry, I'll get you, another shirt'. He refused point blank. He interrogated me further. 'Who are you anyway?' I revealed my identity. He was surprised and then his masculine tone immediately softened. I asked him again, 'Would you like me to get you another shirt?' He withdrew. Then I facetiously tore the whole side of his shirt. I told him that is the kind of punishment you get if you refuse gifts. He laughed and told me I was such a daring little flower.

BENJAMIN: Daring little flower? Aren't those the initials on your sewing machine, your handkerchiefs and gold pendant?

SOPHIE: And pillow. Yes. DLF. I have never forgotten that.

BENJAMIN: He must have worked hard on the farm.

SOPHIE: He earned a pittance. He could just about earn enough to feed himself and his parents and younger sister.

BENJAMIN: Did you go to collect flowers every day?

SOPHIE: Yes. I always enjoyed seeing him. Sometimes he would tell me to go home otherwise Mr Warrington would get angry. Half of the flowerbeds were ruined because of me.

BENJAMIN: Didn't anyone see you?

SOPHIE: We were discreet. Nobody saw us.

BENJAMIN: Did you buy him a shirt, then?

SOPHIE: I bought him a plain blue shirt, nothing over the top.

BENJAMIN: Did he like it?

SOPHIE: He loved it but he was concerned that it wasn't right to accept presents from me.

BENJAMIN: Did he wear it?

SOPHIE: He wrapped it around his body so well. I was simply taken aback and as days went by I discovered, slowly but surely, that I was falling for him.

BENJAMIN: Did you tell him about your feelings?

SOPHIE: No. Of course not. He was from an underprivileged family and I was part of a wealthy empire.
BENJAMIN: Must have been difficult.
SOPHIE: I thought all these silly feelings would flutter away and suddenly one day everything would be back to normal, but each day made my feelings stronger.
BENJAMIN: When did you tell him?
SOPHIE: When I fell over a stupid rusty rake.
BENJAMIN: A rusty rake?
SOPHIE: As usual I was fooling around with him, being sarcastic, playful, flippant. That day when I fell over he came to my rescue. I had hurt my right leg. It was bleeding. He quickly jumped off his tractor and picked me up. I held on tight and he gave me such a wonderful look and radiant smile that I knew at once he felt the same way too.
BENJAMIN: It's great when you discover that glorious moment. I remember that with Michelle.
SOPHIE: He speedily took me to a nearby barn and bandaged my injured leg. He was very sweet and gentle.
BENJAMIN: After that, did you not need to go to hospital?
SOPHIE: After that fate united both hearts.
BENJAMIN: Did anyone from the mansion find out?
SOPHIE: The wrong people found out. Your grandfather was irate and my dearest brother made matters worse. He never was on my side.
BENJAMIN: What happened next?
SOPHIE: I was deeply in love with him and then he started to receive threats. They said they would kill his family if he didn't stop seeing me. Whilst this was going on, my family were mentally torturing me. I was held prisoner in my own home. Never allowed out. Then the worst possible news followed.
BENJAMIN: What?
SOPHIE: I fell pregnant.
BENJAMIN: It must have been quite a shock for you?

SOPHIE: My worst nightmare came true. Christopher had lost his job. His family were told to leave town straightaway. Christopher, sadly, went away with them. It was too late to abort the pregnancy. Well, that is what I told them, but the real purpose of having the baby was so that I would have a part of Christopher with me forever. During my pregnancy I missed Christopher so much. One day he charged into the mansion, declaring his love for me and that he was going to take me away from this bleak mansion. He was wearing the blue shirt that I had given to him. Unfortunately, he was thoroughly beaten. I was so heartbroken. I had witnessed the whole agonising ordeal. They were savage with him and ... I kept loving him.

BENJAMIN: You would think family would stand by you. Especially when it mattered the most. Where was grandma when all this was happening?

SOPHIE: She had been sent home. She was told by my father, literally, 'You are a severe disappointment to this family.' They partially blamed her for my misdemeanour.

BENJAMIN: Did you not fight for him?

SOPHIE: The only other thing left for them to do was to chain me to the walls. Otherwise, security had taken every precaution possible on your grandfather's orders. I had two guards outside my room. Anything I wanted to eat had to be brought up by one of the maids. I was not even permitted to walk around the mansion. My feet were brutally swollen. I had too much water in my body.

BENJAMIN: Did he come back after the beating?

SOPHIE: My father could see how distraught I was with the entire frightful circumstances. I thought at some point maybe, just maybe, he would say to me that everything was all right and that I would be able to see Christopher and be with him for the rest of my life. I was evidently dreaming. Two weeks later – I recall I was six months into my pregnancy – a brown medium-sized package arrived in my name. Inside this package was a white shirt soaked in fresh blood. There was a note. I recognised the handwriting. It read, 'Christopher is no longer alive.' He had been killed. The inscription was in Frederick's handwriting. They were brutal and unrelenting. My heart sank, my whole world fell apart. I felt like a true widow. I never thought he would die. I thought he and I were invincible.

BENJAMIN: And the baby?

SOPHIE: (*sighing heavily*) My delightful son came four weeks early. I was too distressed and suddenly I found myself in labour. The guards summoned the maids and they helped me with my delivery. When he was born he resembled his father. All I could see was Christopher. As I was beginning to recover, the alarming news arrived.

BENJAMIN: What news?

SOPHIE: Three weeks after his birth your dictatorial grandfather deemed it obligatory that I have no connections with a pauper's son. Apparently, our blood was too rich for his veins. (*She begins to cry.*) I was told he would be taken away and be raised by the maids. I wept and wept until I had no energy left. Later on I found out your father had contributed to the suggestion. For three continuous years I cried myself to sleep. I had psychiatrist after psychiatrist come to me but they were unable to soothe me. My cutting pain, my aching wound and my deeply saddened heart never quite recovered. Still to this day I have this ache, this disheartening pain.

BENJAMIN: Where is your son now?

SOPHIE: I'm afraid I can't tell you.

BENJAMIN: Please, Auntie Sophie, please tell me. I swear I will not tell anyone.

SOPHIE: You will be shocked.

BENJAMIN: I am sure it won't be any more shocking than what you have already told me.

SOPHIE: All right, then.

A short silence follows. SOPHIE *gives him a fixed stare.*

BENJAMIN: Auntie Sophie? Auntie Sophie?
SOPHIE: Mmmm?
BENJAMIN: Auntie Sophie?
SOPHIE: Yes? What?
BENJAMIN: Where is your son now? Tell me.
SOPHIE: His name is Peter. Peter Marsh. He is very handsome. I see him every day.
BENJAMIN: Really? Where?
SOPHIE: In this mansion. He is in this tortuous mansion.
BENJAMIN: Peter? Peter? You mean our Peter? The Peter in this mansion?
SOPHIE: Peter, the underbutler, is my son. Because I was crying my heart out your grandfather put forward an agreement. He said I could still be a mother from a distance if I wanted to. As he grew older he was chosen as a minor worker within the mansion. He worked alongside his adopted mother. I had the fortunate task of simply watching from afar. That was better than nothing. However the imperative term in the agreement was that I would never approach Peter as a mother. I would only see him as a member of staff.
BENJAMIN: My goodness me! I just can't believe all this. And all these years you have survived in torment and total silence. You are amazing, Auntie Sophie. You are truly a hero. You carry yourself within society as if all is going well for you. Many people say many things, but really you have a heart of gold. You are truly extraordinary. There are no proper words to describe your bravery and your astonishing endurance. May I suggest something?
SOPHIE: Yes?
BENJAMIN: You must tell him.
SOPHIE: No!
BENJAMIN: You must. He deserves to know his wonderful, caring and sincere mother. Every child deserves to know his mother.

SOPHIE: I can't. Not after all these years. I am confident he will hate me.
BENJAMIN: He will not hate you. He will love you. He is missing you right now. Don't you feel for him?
SOPHIE: I do. I really do.
BENJAMIN: You must tell him. You are responsible for his birth. You did not raise him, I know, but he is yours. He will always be yours. Nothing can mentally divide you. Auntie Sophie, your secret is safe with me. I will not tell anyone, but you must promise me you will inform Peter about the great news. Promise?
SOPHIE: (*a little weepy*) I promise. Thank you, Ben. Thank you for listening.
BENJAMIN: I love you dearly, Auntie Sophie. I hate seeing you like this. I want you to be happy.
SOPHIE: How do I even begin?
BENJAMIN: You must take your time. The right words will come to you. You know it is unbelievably remarkable. Peter is my cousin. Wow! Thank you, Auntie Sophie, for this.

BENJAMIN *puts his arms around* SOPHIE. *She rests her head on his shoulder. They sit in silence.*

SCENE SEVENTEEN

It is late. BENJAMIN *discovers* PETER *sitting idly watching a muted screen.* PETER *is drinking beer out of a can. There are three other cans beside him.*

BENJAMIN: Finding it hard to sleep?
PETER: Master Devereux, what are you doing up so late?
BENJAMIN: Difficulty sleeping.
PETER: Would you like me to get you a beer or something?
BENJAMIN: No thank you. Normally I do not drink at this hour. Is something troubling you?
PETER: Nothing of any great importance.
BENJAMIN: Anything I can help with?
PETER: I hate my job, I hate doing the tedious chores and I am very unhappy with my life. As you can see, nothing of major concern.
BENJAMIN: I see. (*Pause*) How would you want things to be?
PETER: I need my mother. I need to see her. She is responsible for so much. She gave me life and then decided to abandon me. She left me to complete strangers and to this day she has never called or written me a letter to even apologise or ask me how I am. Do you know how that feels?
BENJAMIN: Oh Peter! I was not aware you knew about that.
PETER: All I want is to be loved. I just want to have a mother like everyone else. Is that too much to ask? As far as I'm concerned she is gutless and cruel.
BENJAMIN: Maybe there is a very good explanation.
PETER: There is no explanation! No words can make up for the past twenty-five years. I have friends who think the world of their parents. And what do I have instead? Rita and George!

BENJAMIN: You must not be nasty about them. They have done a very good job of raising you. If they had wanted to, they could have handed you over to another couple. But they didn't. They persevered and let you be the person you are today.
PETER: Wow! And look at me today. I loathe myself and I swing in and out of depression.
BENJAMIN: Then why have you not started looking for your real parents?
PETER: Because they are dead.
BENJAMIN: Who told you that?
PETER: Does it matter?
BENJAMIN: What if your source is incorrect? What if your actual parents are still alive?
PETER: Well, if they were still alive then why on earth have they not shown up on my doorstep? Why have they not bothered to contact me in the last twenty-five years? Am I that awful? Am I the worst son anyone could possibly have?
BENJAMIN: You must not do this. Why are you tormenting yourself? You deserve much more than you think.
PETER: I have been born with the most horrible fate possible. God hates me for sure. Because I have no mother, I find it hard to respect other women. I look at them and use them. I have acquired this awful reputation as a womaniser and who do you think I blame for that? My nuisance of a mother. I attract a woman's attention and then I search for her faults. On finding a superficial flaw I decide, very quickly, to fulfil my physical needs and then I plan the dramatic speech. I successfully dump the girl. I curse my mother for this dispiriting gift. How can I respect women when I have no example to follow?
BENJAMIN: Peter, life is what you make it! If you decide to do something with your time, then you are the one to make that decision, nobody else. It simply is not possible to lay the liability on another's shoulders. To blame your mother is just

a sign of personal weakness. You must not blame her. By doing so, you easily fall into the trap of committing the same mistake again and again.

PETER: What a load of rubbish. Life is not what you make it. If you are destined to have bad luck then no matter how many attempts you have at becoming the best, you eventually fall down the big black hole. (*Pause*) Meesha received a letter this morning from her mother, asking her to go and stay with her for a few days. Her mother sounds like such a sweet person. Why can't my mother write to me like that? Why can't I be called 'sweetheart' and 'pumpkin'? I wish somebody would give me some answers!

BENJAMIN: Well, maybe she is alive and closer than you think.

All of a sudden, AUNTIE SOPHIE *appears. She seems a little fractious.* PETER *and* BENJAMIN *are taken aback.*

PETER: Ms Devereux!

BENJAMIN: Auntie Sophie? What are you doing up at this hour?

SOPHIE: What is going on here? Why are you both up so late? And Peter, why are you drinking beer at this time of night?

PETER: Ms Devereux, we were just talking, that's all.

SOPHIE: About what exactly?

BENJAMIN: Peter was feeling a little down. I thought I would cheer him up.

SOPHIE: Is there any need for it?

BENJAMIN: Auntie Sophie, it's nothing really. You should go to bed.

PETER: Do you need anything at all, Ms Devereux? A glass of cocoa or water perhaps?

SOPHIE: Benjamin, please go to your room now.

BENJAMIN: I will when we have finished chatting.

SOPHIE: Chatting about what? Idle talk serves no purpose. I

implore you to retire to your quarters immediately, before you end up saying something you should not!

BENJAMIN: Auntie Sophie, please let us finish talking. We were only discussing how Peter feels about his employment.

SOPHIE: Sounds to me as if you are covering something up. Maybe something I am not allowed to be a part of?

PETER: The actual truth is I'll be handing in my notice tomorrow, I need to move away from here. I have to find my parents. As I age I know for definite that I will regret not tracking them down.

BENJAMIN: You can't leave us! We need you here. I need you here, and the Dex is fast approaching. We have to make sure all members of staff are present.

SOPHIE: Impossible. I will not have it. We already have a thousand and one things to do and here you are busy wallowing in your empty sorrow. The past is the past. Let it lie. If you find it hard to sleep at night, take some sleeping pills. That way you do not have to think or search for answers. You just lie comfortably until the maids draw your curtains. The call of dawn, I am sure, will instil fresh thoughts. If you continue to speak about past pains, you will only learn to perfect your methods of whingeing and whining.

BENJAMIN: Auntie Sophie, sometimes a man-to-man chat is better than third-party.

PETER: Master Devereux, it's OK.

SOPHIE: Peter, please fetch me a glass of water. Now!

PETER *rushes out of the room on* SOPHIE*'s orders.*

SOPHIE: Do you have any idea what on earth you are doing, Benjamin?

BENJAMIN: I wasn't saying anything untoward.

SOPHIE: Benjamin, I was standing outside listening to your conversation. If you dare to tell him, you will be responsible

for a lot of bloodshed. Did I not stress to you that what we had discussed was confidential?
BENJAMIN: I honestly wasn't going to say anything! I promise.
SOPHIE: I thought I was able to trust you?
BENJAMIN: Why don't you believe me?
SOPHIE: The day he finds out is the day Frederick Devereux will plan my death and bury my body next to Peter's. I do not want that to happen. Silence is golden.
BENJAMIN: Peter is suffering inside. Surely he has a right to know?
SOPHIE: Peter's suffering should be seen as a blessing in disguise. By enduring past anguish he is still able to live a normal and sensible life. The moment the heartbreaking truth is revealed, his days will be numbered.
BENJAMIN: Auntie Sophie, I promise you, I will never utter a single word. I do not want to lose you or Peter. Doesn't it hurt you when he talks about his suffering like that?
SOPHIE: More than you can imagine. My world is very small and exceptionally sensitive. I have my own flesh and blood under my nose but I have no right to be his mother. (*sighing deeply*) Goodnight, Benjamin. Guard my secret with your life.
BENJAMIN: I love you, Auntie Sophie. You are a good person. Things will change one day, you'll see.

AUNTIE SOPHIE *exits.* PETER *arrives with a glass of water.*

PETER: Is everything all right? I came as quickly as I could.
BENJAMIN: Peter, you must stay. You just have to. I will not let you hand in your resignation under any circumstances!
PETER: Didn't she want her glass of water?
BENJAMIN: I thought she should really go to bed. She was very tired.
PETER: Sometimes she can be rather scary.

BENJAMIN: So are you serious about handing in your notice?
PETER: I'm sure there will be many applicants for the position.
BENJAMIN: Peter, you will remain here and that is final. You do not need to move away. And besides, the maids will miss you. Father will wonder why and what about your current girlfriend? She'll be wondering why you eloped without her?
PETER: It's called flirting and having a laugh. It is never serious. Your father will never wonder why. He would not care in the slightest. If you don't mind my saying, he has no idea about how to treat people. He has a very devious mind and likes hurting people, especially members of his family. It is second nature to him. For example, your father is accusing Master Thomas Devereux of stealing the sum of £7000 from the family safe, but the fact of the matter is he actually stole it himself.
BENJAMIN: That sounds too far-fetched to be true.
PETER: I saw him do it. He thought nobody was there, but I saw him with my own eyes. As I bent down to get rid of this stain underneath his bureau, I heard him stomp into the room and go directly to the safe. He opened it, counted the money and put the banknotes in a blue and white bag. Then he went out for the whole afternoon and did not return until dinner was served. He was obviously up to something.
BENJAMIN: Are you very certain about your facts?
PETER: I swear. There is no reason for me to lie. I just feel sorry for your poor mother, who has to put up with such a demeaning and tyrannical human being.
BENJAMIN: Why would he do such a thing?
PETER: I don't know. The whole incident seems extremely odd.
BENJAMIN: But it just doesn't make sense!
PETER: Your father certainly works in mysterious ways. Remember, I was not the one who told you this.
BENJAMIN: Does anyone else know?

PETER: Only Coral and Meesha and half my village.
BENJAMIN: Oh!
PETER: Your father is a frightening man. No one would dare say anything. They do not want to die before they have to.
BENJAMIN: Does Auntie Sophie scare you?
PETER: Your Auntie Sophie seems to live in a world of her own. Her selfish and pompous nature proves how self-centred and rude she is. Good job she never married nor had any children. I am sure they would have hated her.
BENJAMIN: Peter, I really think you should stop there.
PETER: I appreciate your genuine concern, but I just hate working here.
BENJAMIN: Well on that note, I think it wise that you and I should part.
PETER: But it is the truth.
BENJAMIN: Beer cans are subject to debate.
PETER: I am not speaking under the influence of alcohol, I can assure you!
BENJAMIN: We can only determine that the next day. See how you feel when dawn breaks and how much you are able to recall.
PETER: I will hand in my notice as soon as possible, you'll see.
BENJAMIN: Goodnight, Peter. Make sure you get rid of those beer cans safely and please refrain from drinking at this time of night in future. It is not good for the soul.
PETER: Goodnight, Master Devereux. By the time I see you again, I will be carrying my bags home.
BENJAMIN: I shall look forward to that hour. When fish grow wings you will leave this mansion.

BENJAMIN *exits as* PETER *looks on.*

SCENE EIGHTEEN

RAISOR *appears, walking down the street. He is smartly dressed in a brown threadbare suit for his date with* LUCY. *He masters a swanky walk with his head lifted up high. He spots* BENJAMIN *from afar and rushes to catch up with him.*

RAISOR: Ah, Master Benjamin, what do you think?
BENJAMIN: Very impressive. Who is the lucky girl?
RAISOR: Lucy Hopkins. The beautiful flower girl in Franco's Valley. She fancies me. And I actually have the hots for her as well. She has the most gorgeous eyes I have ever seen.
BENJAMIN: Well, that's refreshingly reassuring. What have you planned then? Where are you taking her?
RAISOR: Well, I was hoping that she would make a suggestion. I just want to be near her and look at her and smell her.
BENJAMIN: Don't you think at least you should have a back-up plan yourself?
RAISOR: Well my back-up plan is just ... you know ... you know?
BENJAMIN: What?
RAISOR: I'm going to use my hormones and that's all. I have no intention of using my brain.
BENJAMIN: What if you scare her?
RAISOR: I won't. I will start off by talking about the weather, the stars and her sparkling eyes. Then maybe the moon and the autumn breeze. And then I will play her my mixed tape. (*Drawing out an audio cassette.*) It's got a few love songs on it. We'll dance, I'll look into her eyes and then her blouse and by then I should have gained my rightful entry.

BENJAMIN: I'm afraid I am rather concerned about your methods.
RAISOR: Hey, it worked four years ago so I don't see why it wouldn't work now.
BENJAMIN: Now and four years ago, there is quite a difference.
RAISOR: As long as I look irresistible I have no issue.
BENJAMIN: Shouldn't you talk about feelings first? Women like that sort of thing.
RAISOR: And ruin the moment? No chance.
BENJAMIN: Raisor, you should be careful not to offend her.
RAISOR: I'm not going to do that. I just want nature to take its course. I'm not going to interrupt the rhythm of pulling power.
BENJAMIN: Make sure you take it slowly.
RAISOR: I won't rip her clothes off. I'll undo them politely. I do get stuck with belts, though, so I might ask her to unbuckle that herself.
BENJAMIN: Raisor, I think you are jumping ahead. You must be able to respect her wishes. If she says she just wants to talk then you have to accept that. Some women are shy at first, others like to talk. On first dates you should be making a good impression. You should be kind, considerate, polite and friendly.
RAISOR: Master Benjamin, look, I don't know how to read fancy books, so what you're saying to me obviously makes no sense. Lucy only went to school for about six months, so I know she will welcome my methods kind-heartedly. I think book methods should be used on people who read those books.
BENJAMIN: I suppose you have a point.
RAISOR: My approach is more personal and physical. I happen to be quite a good mover.
BENJAMIN: You see, if I did that with my girlfriend, she would probably get very upset and never want to see me again.

RAISOR: Your girlfriend? You still have a girlfriend?
BENJAMIN: Pardon me? Of course I have a girlfriend. I'm sure you all know about Michelle. It seems to be the talk of the town.
RAISOR: You don't seem very bitter.
BENJAMIN: About what?
RAISOR: Your girlfriend. Don't you miss her at all?
BENJAMIN: Of course I do. I like being with her. I enjoy her company. She makes me very happy.
RAISOR: But you can't do that anymore.
BENJAMIN: Why not?
RAISOR: Because she recently became . . . are you sure you don't know?
BENJAMIN: Raisor, what are you getting at, spit it out?
RAISOR: Michelle has gone away.
BENJAMIN: Where?
RAISOR: To God.
BENJAMIN: To God?
RAISOR: She's decided to start her life beyond the stars and mix with the angels.
BENJAMIN: Have you been drinking again?
RAISOR: No. I only do that in the evenings or when I have some money or if I have stolen somebody's wallet.
BENJAMIN: Raisor, what are you actually saying?
RAISOR: Your girlfriend? Have you seen her since Sunday?
BENJAMIN: No.
RAISOR: That's because she's decided to pass away.
BENJAMIN: What!
RAISOR: It was by accident of course. Not planned at all.

Suddenly JIM *appears. He approaches both of them in a breathless, rush. He gestures vociferously at* RAISOR *and tries to confuse him.* BENJAMIN *is quite bemused.*

JIM: There you are! I've been looking for you everywhere.

BENJAMIN: Jim, what is Raisor going on about? Is it true about Michelle?
JIM: Raisor always seems to be in a world of his own. You must not take him seriously.
RAISOR: Tell him, Jim, tell him that we made a mistake.
JIM: Let's go now. You've said quite enough already. And besides, Lucy must be waiting for you.
BENJAMIN: No! Just wait a minute! Are you trying to tell me that you both had something to do with Michelle passing away?
RAISOR: Yes!
JIM: No! No! No! We really must go now.
BENJAMIN: Why? Did someone tell you to do it?
JIM: It's not our place to say.
BENJAMIN: I demand that you clearly state the truth and no beating around the bush.
RAISOR: I did. We, by pure mistake, put too much pressure on the shovel. Jim was supposed to do it delicately. He's only used to badgering fierce animals.
JIM: Shut up, you old fool!
BENJAMIN: So you did kill her? You admit it?
RAISOR: As I said, we made an awful mistake. But she did look beautiful if that's any consolation.
JIM: Raisor, let's go! How many times have I told you not to talk about work-related matters? It is very unprofessional.

JIM *pulls* RAISOR *over to his side very hard and directs him towards a nearby alley.* BENJAMIN *is left astounded.*

SCENE NINETEEN

All members of the DEVEREUX *family are gathered in a conference room.* FREDERICK *is sitting down behind a large oval table. Alongside him are* SOPHIE, NANCY *and* PENELOPE. THOMAS *and* BENJAMIN *remain standing with the mansion staff;* PENCHARD *is also present.*

FREDERICK: I am pleased to see that you all managed to attend this meeting. As you all clearly know, the Dex is tomorrow.
THOMAS: So what? Hardly electrifying!
FREDERICK: I expect everybody to be on their best behaviour. Under no circumstances should there be any humiliation, disturbance of any kind or any form of rudeness, especially from Thomas. Do you understand that, Thomas? No ill-mannered behaviour, no bursting out loudly and no drunken talk will be acceptable.
THOMAS: Whatever, Father! Whatever pleases your shallow, sanctimonious and supercilious self.
FREDERICK: Thomas, stop acting like a fool! I will not tolerate such foul behaviour. You know how important this event is. You know it is essential that everything works out perfectly!
BENJAMIN: So did you have something to do with her death?
FREDERICK: What on earth are you babbling on about, boy?!
BENJAMIN: You seem to be the mastermind behind her demise.
FREDERICK: I do not have adequate patience to listen to gibberish. I am here purely to stipulate a paramount purpose. The Dex. You are all to be extremely hospitable and tactful.

You will not take offence at other guests' impertinence, even if it is truly abominable. They will be our guests and we will take good care of them. Dress code, as usual, impeccable smartness. No bright or clashing colours. I will not permit any peculiar forms of dress sense. Elegant, conservative and pleasantly fashionable. You will also wear a magnetic smile. No miserable or perturbed faces. You will not speak about your own distress, you will not share any current anguish. We are a contented and perfect family. Our luxurious lifestyles are the envy of many people. I would like the satisfying myth to remain that way. Jack Haddy, our superlative and assiduous Dex organiser has arranged all necessary amenities. If you do have any further queries please contact him, and then he will approach me if needed. I shall be extremely busy for the next twenty-four hours. So please do not come to me unless there is an unavoidable crisis.

THOMAS: You mean like fire or theft or burglary or stealing from the family safe or planning and committing a cold-blooded murder or dying in an accident?

FREDERICK: I only have time for sensible questions.

BENJAMIN: If I find out that it was your fault I will kill you. You have utterly destroyed my life.

FREDERICK: Ben, keep your voice down unless you wish me to call security.

BENJAMIN: I detest the sight of you, Father!

SOPHIE: Please keep these resentful comments to yourself. Calm down.

PENELOPE: Father, allow me to commend you for your cruelty, insensitivity and rudeness. You clearly champion all those traits beautifully.

FREDERICK: That is quite enough, young lady!

PENELOPE: I have invited Daniel Sullivan and a friend to the Dex.

FREDERICK: Penchard, please make sure security have been

warned regarding Daniel's description. On his arrival he is to be thrown out. His silly and pathetic friend can watch.

PENCHARD: As you wish, sir.

THOMAS: Daniel should be allowed to attend the Dex. After all, he is family.

FREDERICK: Am I the only one with any sanity in this room?!

NANCY: Thomas was only joking, Father.

FREDERICK: His ridiculous jokes are not normal jokes. They are offensive. You are no son of mine!

SOPHIE: No need to raise your tone, Frederick! The boy has a different manner of thinking.

FREDERICK: Why does everything go wrong? Why is there no decorum within this family! Why am I made out to be the villain here? I have tried very hard to be a loving, attentive and sincere parent. You all seem to misunderstand my paternal nature. Due to that misjudgement, you are disrespectful towards me. I realise that anything and almost everything I say is taken as a bitter pill, but I am who I am and when I pass away you will start to value my opinions.

NANCY: Father, please don't get so angry. We are all here today in this room because we care. If we didn't care we would not bother.

FREDERICK: Coral, Meesha, Peter, Rose and Patrick, you all know your duties. Please make sure you carry them out successfully. Any slip-ups and I will be very cross, and you may all end up looking for another job. I hope you will not let me down. On that note, I wish to end this protracted discussion. I will see you all tomorrow in good spirits.

FREDERICK *rises and exits abruptly.*

SCENE TWENTY

The Dex. The most prestigious and glamorous event in the Devereux calendar. The Devereux mansion has been polished from top to bottom. The grand and magnificent ballroom boasts breathtaking adornment. An extravagant and colourful staging area has been assembled. The ballroom is festooned with flowers. There are vast rows of tables full of many culinary delights. Great volumes of champagne and other drinks have been arranged at the centre of the hall. The illuminated crystal chandeliers spread an eye-catching glitter around the room. The spotlights centre on the massive dance floor. The many guests start pouring in, all in their superb finery. There is a buzzing of conversation, music and patterns of loud laughter. All members of the Devereux family are dressed in elegant attire. Some are enjoying themselves more than others.
BENJAMIN DEVEREUX *looks out of place. He seems tired and a touch lugubrious. As he stands alone drinking some tropical punch, he is approached by a beautiful, tall, dark young lady.*

ESTONIA: You must be Benjamin Devereux? (*She extends her hand.*)
BENJAMIN: (*He does not reciprocate.*) Yes. And you are?
ESTONIA: Estonia Darvel.
BENJAMIN: Estonia? As in the country?
ESTONIA: I was conceived in Estonia.
BENJAMIN: How touching!
ESTONIA: You seem rather preoccupied.
BENJAMIN: The Dex means very little to me.
ESTONIA: But it is a great excuse to have a party.
BENJAMIN: Whatever thrills you!
ESTONIA: You should have invited some of your friends.

BENJAMIN: Maybe.
ESTONIA: You look very smart.
BENJAMIN: It's only a tedious requirement. I am expected to display this sort of effort. Please do not think or even assume I have willingly shown up. I do have far better things to do than waste time with a bunch of affluent and ignorant bodies.
ESTONIA: Ouch! What is eating at you? I'm only trying to be nice. I mean no harm or insult. (*Pause*) Take a deep breath.
BENJAMIN: Pardon?
ESTONIA: Just do it. Look into my eyes. Look. (*She gestures*) Breath in, breath out and release all your negative energy bit by bit. Feel the tension diving to the lowest point possible. Feel the freedom. Does that help?
BENJAMIN: I suppose it makes me feel different.
ESTONIA: Good. Now can we have a sensible conversation? Hi, I'm Estonia Darvel. I run my own media company.
BENJAMIN: What type of media company?
ESTONIA: Ever heard of *Browbeat* magazine?
BENJAMIN: Yes. I believe I have bought copies in the past.
ESTONIA: I am the sole founder and head honcho of *Browbeat*.
BENJAMIN: Wow! Must be very interesting, no doubt demanding.
ESTONIA: And you? What about you?
BENJAMIN: I seem to hold a thorny status within my family. I only resemble pain to my father and I appear to be too cavalier with his money.
ESTONIA: I'm very sorry to hear that.
BENJAMIN: So do you have someone? You know a worthy companion?
ESTONIA: No. Not yet. You?
BENJAMIN: A very sore and stinging wound.
ESTONIA: There were rumours, of course.
BENJAMIN: My glass is now my only friend.
ESTONIA: Must be hard.
BENJAMIN: So do you know everyone here?

ESTONIA: Majority. See that guy over there, dark beard, green tie?

BENJAMIN: Yes?

ESTONIA: He just came out of jail six weeks ago. Apparently he assaulted his secretary.

BENJAMIN: Really?

ESTONIA: She took him to court and then put him in prison, only to discover that she had actually fallen in love with him. So she decided to get him out. Naturally, in the beginning he was devastated with the ruling. She lied about the whole thing.

BENJAMIN: Why would she do that?

ESTONIA: Money. She asked for a pay rise and he refused. So she decided to get nasty.

BENJAMIN: Hardly seems fair.

ESTONIA: Injustice sometimes is peace of mind. See that bald chap over there? Mr Duke Fresner. He sells tobacco. He's made a fortune! He has vacation homes all over the world. I think his most recent purchase was a villa in Kenya.

BENJAMIN: Kenya?

ESTONIA: Never been to Kenya. You?

BENJAMIN: No, closest for me is South Africa.

ESTONIA: Then we have Lady Vanessa Pout. She is the cosmetics queen.

BENJAMIN: Yes, I have heard of her.

ESTONIa: She makes a million a month.

BENJAMIN: The taxman must like her then.

ESTONIA: She's married to one. Her husband helps her dodge a few hundred thousand here and there. You see Martin Feathercroft over there?

BENJAMIN: Yes, the most devious swindler of our time.

ESTONIA: Are you familiar with Ashley Boates?

BENJAMIN: Ashley Boates, oh, the father of eighteen illegitimate children, and he sold two of them in North America.

ESTONIA: Martin Feathercroft bought one of them.
BENJAMIN: Really?
ESTONIA: He's called him Chase Feathercroft. He's at boarding school now.
BENJAMIN: Chase must be very confused.
ESTONIA: He was last seen in a public house.
BENJAMIN: How old is he?
ESTONIA: He's only fifteen!
BENJAMIN: Oh! You notice that woman with the large meringue hat?
ESTONIA: Yes?
BENJAMIN: Do you know who she is?
ESTONIA: She's the pearl queen. If you ever need pearls, she's the lady to contact. Pearls Harbour she calls it.
BENJAMIN: Calls what?
ESTONIA: Her bijouterie.

THOMAS *appears from behind them carrying two drinks in each hand. He is slightly tipsy.*

THOMAS: Bloody awful crowd! All they talk about is money. I wish they'd all shut up and go home. Ben, aren't you going to introduce me?
BENJAMIN: This is Estonia Darvel. Estonia, this is...
ESTONIA: Thomas Devereux, your brother. Yes, I do know.
THOMAS: From the way you look I would say you seem a little shallow, young lady!
ESTONIA: I beg your pardon!
BENJAMIN: Sorry, he must be a little intoxicated.
THOMAS: I am not drunk. The ambience in here could make anyone feel the same way as I'm feeling. It's too heavy for my liking.
BENJAMIN: Thomas, don't have any more champagne, OK.
THOMAS: Stop telling me what to do! (*He turns towards* ESTONIA.) So do you want to dance?

ESTONIA: No thank you!
THOMAS: Stop being so annoying! (*He passes his drinks to* BENJAMIN *and grabs* ESTONIA*'s arm.*) Come on! I have no intention of liking you. I am already spoken for. Her name is Josie. She is prettier than you. Anyway, come on then.

THOMAS *almost lifts her up and pushes her onto the dance floor.*

ESTONIA: How dare you!
THOMAS: My manners will surface, just give them time.
ESTONIA: Benjamin, help me!
BENJAMIN: He really means no harm. Just relax.

As THOMAS *whisks her off, a gigantic masculine figure approaches.* BEN *looks up.* MR FRANK MOLLOY *appears. He is very pale and carries a rather aggressive demeanour. He speaks with a deep voice.*

FRANK: Benjamin Devereux (*He grabs his hand and starts shaking it vigorously.*) I have heard the marvellous news. You must be delighted.
BENJAMIN: I'm sorry?
FRANK: Ah, you modest little boy. Your father has told me the great news. You certainly are a lucky boy.
BENJAMIN: What did he tell you?
FRANK: Now, don't be shy. You know she is very beautiful.
BENJAMIN: I am sorry to sound so rude but what are you talking about and above all who are you?

FREDERICK DEVEREUX *appears from the crowd and joins in the conversation.*

FREDERICK: Ah! There you are Ben! This is Mr Frank Molloy. He's too rich for his own good. He simply has too much money! (*He bursts into laughter.*)

BENJAMIN: How awful for you!
FRANK: Oh goodness me, Fred, you didn't tell me you had a joker for a son!
BENJAMIN: Hardly amusing!

FREDERICK *and* FRANK *let out a raucous laugh.*

FRANK: So when is the big day, Fred? I hope it's before my yachting exhibition.
FREDERICK: Don't worry, we will be sending out the invitations soon. You're going to love it. Hope Lara will make it?
FRANK: I'm sure she will be only too pleased to attend. She loves weddings.
BENJAMIN: What wedding?
FREDERICK: Frank, let us examine the speech list. I want you to verify a few details. Shall we go and get a few nibbly bits first?
BENJAMIN: I demand to know what you are talking about?
FREDERICK: Ben, we don't have time to explain. There are many other guests who require my attention. We can by all means talk about it later on. Now go and cheerfully mingle with the rest of the wealthy crowd.
BENJAMIN: Whose wedding is it, Father?

FREDERICK *and* FRANK *completely ignore* BENJAMIN*'s question.* BENJAMIN *becomes rather bemused.* ESTONIA *returns.*

ESTONIA: Is your brother receiving medical assistance?
BENJAMIN: Why were they talking about a wedding?
ESTONIA: Surely he is in need of professional help? Alcohol is certainly not the correct form of therapy.
BENJAMIN: Why should I be excited about a wedding that I don't even have knowledge of?

ESTONIA: Why does he have to be so pushy and, my goodness me, he has mouth freshness issues!
BENJAMIN: He said I am a lucky boy. Why would he say that?
ESTONIA: And why was he carrying a sponge?
BENJAMIN: Father must be up to something.
ESTONIA: He kept sniffing it from time to time. There's definitely something wrong with him.
BENJAMIN: Do you know anything about a damned wedding?
ESTONIA: What wedding?
BENJAMIN: My father is going to be sending out invitations soon.
ESTONIA: Oh! I know what he is talking about. Oh, you poor soul! You poor little love!
BENJAMIN: Excuse me? Poor little love? Nobody ever said that to me except Michelle.
ESTONIA: Yes, and of course poor Michelle. She was a person who stumbled over unfortunate circumstances.
BENJAMIN: As you can imagine, the news of her supposedly accidental death has totally destroyed my dream of an honest and happy life.
ESTONIA: Well, once the dust settles and time begins to heal the ugliness of the past, you will once again smell the splendid scent of happiness. Why are you looking at me like that? I thought you knew.
BENJAMIN: Cryptic talk is a form of harassment. Could you please get to the bloody point?!
ESTONIA: Strong language won't make it any quicker! Do you like me?
BENJAMIN: Is it relevant that I answer?
ESTONIA: Please?
BENJAMIN: You look all right on the outside, but the crucial question is what's on the inside. You could be a horrible person or very nice.
ESTONIA: I can assure you I have great qualities, a great family, wonderful friends and a superb career. I would not have those unless I was a good person.

BENJAMIN: Fair point! (*Pause*) Was there something else?
ESTONIA: I need a more direct response.
BENJAMIN: You scare me, quite frankly.
ESTONIA: I'm sure that means you like me.
BENJAMIN: I've just experienced a dreadful and heartbreaking loss, I have no intention of pursuing any other relationship.
ESTONIA: All the more reason to be with someone. Come on, let's go out and see the fireworks. I hate this melancholic ambience.
BENJAMIN: Just a minute. Of all people, why are you being friendly?
ESTONIA: You still don't get it, do you?
BENJAMIN: Get what? I loathe all this suspense! Now, for the hundredth time, who the hell is getting married?
ESTONIA: It's us silly! I'm going to be your beautiful new bride. I'm just so happy.

BENJAMIN *is astounded. He becomes frozen with disbelief.*

ESTONIA: So you really didn't know about the wedding? Oh, it's going to be incredible. Estonia Maria Devereux. I have always dreamt of marrying into a gracious, honourable and opulent family. My parents are ever so thrilled. I must say I believe that true companionship will blossom between us and that will lead to such pure and admirable love. I will always look toward you with loving eyes and speak highly of you. My brother Lorenzo will be present at the wedding. He should be coming over for four weeks. Shall we walk to the firework display, then.
BENJAMIN: I feel nauseous.
ESTONIA: I think you need fresh air, it's quite stuffy in here. Come on, let's get out of here.

ESTONIA *puts her arm around* BEN *and they exit.*

SCENE TWENTY-ONE

All the guests are now gathered for the renowned speeches. JACK HADDY, *the organiser, begins the inaugural ceremony.*

JACK: Ladies and gentlemen, if I could please have your attention. Thank you. First of all, I would like you all to raise your glasses and congratulate Mr Devereux once again for such a brilliant and auspicious occasion. I am certain you will agree that there simply is no other event that exhilarates us more.
ALL: Here! Here! To Mr Devereux.

They all raise their glasses. Loud applause follows the toast. MR DEVEREUX *is standing beside* JACK HADDY *and he acknowledges the crowd by taking a slight bow.*

JACK: I thank you all for your kindness. It is such a wonderful spectacle to see such rich and beautiful faces here today (*some laughter*). The Devereux Extravaganza is the most exceptional and sensational event of the calendar year. The Dex believes in true business opportunities. As long as we are guided through respectable and legitimate commerce we can all look forward to thrilling opportunities, potential expansion and successful mergers. We seek the adventurous and perspicacious minds and we seek the dauntless and industrious bodies. Their eminent efforts and notable financial backgrounds deliver noteworthy products that you and I are able to verify and be influenced by. Those who are hesitant and reticent we have no room for. The vast business world demands courage and diligence. Today we are all celebrating that particular joy of achievement. We share this immense success. Our bright futures are prime examples and set new, exciting trends in career pursuits within our exclusive industries. In the words of the gracious Mr Charles Fielding, who attended the Dex last year, 'The money we make proves that we exert ourselves with blood and sweat.' Another important axiom provided by the Late Mr Peter Winchesterton, may he rest in peace, reads as follows, 'Our mighty wealth reveals that we are not lazy. To inherit it you cannot gloat, to labour for it you can perfectly exult.' And that is what we are doing today.

THOMAS: Oh, get on with it! Please!

The crowd are stunned.

JACK: (*trying to ignore the interruption*)　We ... ladies and gentlemen, we will now hear and show appreciation of these specific marvellous examples. Our initial guest list ...

THOMAS: Stinks!

JACK: Our initial guest list boasts two distinguished male figures. Ladies and gentlemen, allow me to introduce Mr Frank Molloy of Molloy Shipping and Yachting and Hansel Maynard of Maynard Universal Jinx. I firmly assure you ... you will be thoroughly impressed.

THOMAS: What a load of nonsense! All they talk about is their self-centred universe. Oh, I'm bored, I'm going to bed. Any more champagne, send it to my room.

The crowd is aghast. FREDERICK *rises from his seat. He is irate. He stomps over to* THOMAS *and follows him out of the hall.*

JACK: Please accept our sincere and heartfelt apologies, ladies and gentlemen. A very minor hiccup. Rest assured we will experience no further insolent delays. Please remain content. Mr Devereux will rejoin us shortly. He would not willingly miss any part of the grand presentation. I genuinely thank you for your understanding and valuable patience. Let us continue. Please put your hands together for the fabulously gifted Mr Frank Molloy.

As everyone applauds, the presentation ceremony commences. NANCY *and* BENJAMIN *are seated in the crowd and they quietly discuss a few things.*

NANCY: Poor old Frank has put on an awful amount of weight, hasn't he?
BENJAMIN: Too much of the good life!
NANCY: He almost looks like a bear!
BENJAMIN: I wonder what Father is saying to Thomas?
NANCY: Maybe he's getting the large padlock out. Sometimes Thomas does the silliest things.
BENJAMIN: I hate the Dex. I must admit I agree with Thomas. This is really boring.
NANCY: How long do you think until I get stupidly drunk?
BENJAMIN: Another hour perhaps? I'll join you.
NANCY: Thomas is funny.
BENJAMIN: He has more courage than all of us put together.
NANCY: Auntie Sophie seems deeply upset and isolated over there. Do you think I should go and talk to her?
BENJAMIN: No, don't worry. She'll be fine. I am sure it is nothing dramatic. She is solid as a rock.
NANCY: I heard that reporter really dug his heels in.
BENJAMIN: He's covering the story on the Dex. He's sitting right at the back.
NANCY: Hasn't he finished yet?
BENJAMIN: Do you know Estonia Darvel?
NANCY: Yes and you're welcome.
BENJAMIN: So she was your dim-witted and hurtful idea?
NANCY: It's called the healing process.
BENJAMIN: You know very well that I will not go ahead with it.

NANCY: But we don't want you to go ahead with it. Initially. Give it time and it will sink in and then we will rejoice together.
BENJAMIN: If you can be shrewd then so can I. I am really getting fed up with this family's astute games and destructive lies.
NANCY: Anger would be the first stage.
BENJAMIN: No wonder Thomas is totally messed up!
NANCY: What's the time?
BENJAMIN: Time this whole thing was over.
NANCY: I think it's time for some action.
BENJAMIN: I thought Father would have returned by now. He must be really angry.
NANCY: (*rising*) I wonder if he will be back at all? Excuse me.
BENJAMIN: (*moving back a little*) Don't be long. I don't want to be sitting here alone with these goons.
NANCY: There will be a reason for my late return.
BENJAMIN: Well, then, I'm coming too.
NANCY: No, you must not! Just sit down and wait.
BENJAMIN: I'll go to Mum then. I'm going to find her.
NANCY: Just sit still. Everything will be clear in a moment.
BENJAMIN: If only there was some form of entertainment.
NANCY: You want entertainment? I can give you that.
BENJAMIN: Are you going to sing?
NANCY: Even better. I intend to recreate history. Memorable history.

As NANCY *exits* PENELOPE *approaches* BENJAMIN.

PENELOPE: Have you seen Daniel?
BENJAMIN: No.
PENELOPE: I have been waiting down at the west-wing archway for the last half hour. I wonder where he is.
BENJAMIN: Maybe Father's killed him without your knowing. He did warn you.

PENELOPE: If Father lays one finger on him then I'm going to run away and leave town for good.
BENJAMIN: Penny I think Meesha's calling you.

PENELOPE *quickly runs over.* MEESHA *hands her a note. As* PENELOPE *reads the note she becomes tearful.* BENJAMIN *rushes to her side.*

BENJAMIN: What's the matter? What's happened?
PENELOPE: He's gone. He's been told to leave town.
BENJAMIN: Let me see the note.
PENELOPE: (*She hands the note to him.*) My nightmare has begun all over again. If only there was something I could do.
BENJAMIN: Father never ceases to amaze me.
PENELOPE: I hate Father, I hate this stupid mansion and everything about it. (*She lets out a growl.*)
BENJAMIN: I thought you had an invincible plan.
PENELOPE: We talked all night about this and how everything would be fine from now on. We had so much to look forward to.
BENJAMIN: Nancy's big mouth got you into trouble.
PENELOPE: I can't put up with this anymore. I am going to put an end to all this.
BENJAMIN: Where are you going?
PENELOPE: I am going to talk to Father and straighten out a few things for good. Enough is enough. I might have to teach him a lesson or two. Who does he think he is!
BENJAMIN: Let me come with you. I'm sure I have plenty to contribute to the discussion.

BENJAMIN *and* PENELOPE *exit.*

SCENE TWENTY-TWO

BENJAMIN *and* PENELOPE *spot* AUNTIE SOPHIE *pacing up and down the hallway. She is a little startled on seeing their approach.*

BENJAMIN: What are you doing here, Auntie Sophie?
SOPHIE: I needed some air. I've got a lot on my mind.
PENELOPE: Father has driven Daniel away with his horrid threats. Meesha passed on this note to me. Look.
SOPHIE: (*She takes the note and looks at it briefly.*)   Oh my goodness! He's used very harmful language indeed.
PENELOPE: But I love him. I want to be with him.
BENJAMIN: Where is Father? Is he in his study?
SOPHIE: No! You mustn't go in there!
BENJAMIN: Why not?
SOPHIE: Frederick has . . . told me not to disturb him. Earlier I did go in there but then he told me to wait outside. He was acting rather odd.
PENELOPE: What is he doing?
SOPHIE: I think he is talking to Rose.
BENJAMIN: Rose? That's not possible. A few minutes ago I saw her wheeling in two large trays of salmon bites and beluga caviar.
SOPHIE: Oh! Perhaps I'm confusing her with someone else.
PENELOPE: Look there's some red ribbon sticking out from under the door.
SOPHIE: Please don't touch that!
BENJAMIN: Goodness me Auntie Sophie! You seem awfully jumpy. Are you all right?

SOPHIE: I just feel a little uneasy at the moment. Maybe it's my stomach.
PENELOPE: I wonder how that ribbon got there.
SOPHIE: Perhaps it did belong to someone and it accidentally caught on to something without their knowing.
BENJAMIN: Auntie Sophie, if you wouldn't mind, could we go in before you? We need to speak to Father urgently.

There is a sudden cry for help. THOMAS *is yelling out from behind a closed door. They all rush to the end of the hallway. The door is locked.*

BENJAMIN: Is that you Thomas?
THOMAS: Get me out of here!
PENELOPE: Oh you poor thing! What has Father done to you?
THOMAS: He's bruised my face and arm. I did say that I was sorry. He wouldn't listen. Let me out please? I promise I'll behave.
BENJAMIN: Do you know where the spare key would be?
SOPHIE: Penchard must have one somewhere.
THOMAS: I need to go to the toilet as well. I think I've had too much to drink.
BENJAMIN: Even if I summon Penchard he is not going to oblige.
PENELOPE: The only other option is to break down the door. Thomas, can you find something large and heavy in there?
THOMAS: No, not really. There's only an old cupboard and sofa in here. I can't lift them.
SOPHIE: Thomas, dear, be patient. I'll go and search Penchard's den. I am sure I'll be able to locate the key in there.

SOPHIE *exits.*

THOMAS: He yelled at me so much that I couldn't get a word

in edgeways. He grabbed me tightly and shook me. He told me that I was an utter disgrace and I should always be locked up. Then he pushed me back so hard that I fell to the ground and hurt my knee. He is so mean. He said he is going to send me off to an institution and never allow me to return home. If only Mummy was here. She would have fought my corner.
PENELOPE: Yes. If only she was here. She would have liked Daniel. She would have completely understood my feelings.
THOMAS: Mummy is here with us today.
BENJAMIN: Yes. Her spirit lives on.
THOMAS: No. What I meant was she is here.
BENJAMIN: Everybody knows that is not possible.
THOMAS: But she must be here because I saw her. When I visited her yesterday, she told me this year was going to be a special year.
BENJAMIN: I realise you speak to her more than anybody else but this kind of talk shows you're insane.
THOMAS: She is here. If you don't believe me then see for yourself. She is here at the Dex.
PENELOPE: Thomas, she is dead. She can't attend the Dex because Mummy is not alive. Oh you poor thing!
THOMAS: I know what I saw. I have only had six or seven glasses of champagne.
BENJAMIN: Oh dear! The drink explains it all.
PENELOPE: I wonder if Auntie Sophie has had any luck with the key.
THOMAS: You needn't worry any further. I don't need to go to the toilet anymore.
PENELOPE: Oh Thomas! You filthy man!
THOMAS: I'll have to throw these trousers away.
BENJAMIN: If Auntie Sophie does not return soon I'll have to knock the door down.
PENELOPE: Oh look! The red ribbon has disappeared. Someone must have pulled it from the other side.

BENJAMIN: I must say Father is spending a lot of time in there. He's missing all the speeches and presentations.
PENELOPE: That doesn't seem right. He never misses a minute of the Dex.
BENJAMIN: He's beginning to worry me.
PENELOPE: Thomas, hold on for a bit. We're going to check Father's study.

PENCHARD *arrives with an exasperated look.*

PENCHARD: Where is Mr Devereux? Have you seen him?
BENJAMIN: He's in his study. Penny and I were about to check on him.
PENCHARD: (*He knocks on the door.*) Mr Devereux, are you in there? (*He turns the door handle. It is locked.*) He never locks this door. What on earth is going on?
BENJAMIN: I'm going in. Step back.

BENJAMIN *kicks down the door. The door bangs open. They discover* FREDERICK DEVEREUX*'s body on the floor with bloody stab wounds.*

PENELOPE: Oh my God! What's going on? What's the matter with Father? Why is there so much blood? Ben, why is Father bleeding like this?
BENJAMIN: I cannot believe this! He has been stabbed!
PENELOPE: Ben, he's dead, isn't he? He's dead. Someone's killed him. (*She kneels beside the body. She is crying.*) He's left us.
BENJAMIN: I wonder if his heart is still beating. (*He places an ear on Frederick's chest.*) No. There's nothing there. I can't hear anything. Oh wait a minute! No. No. He is no longer with us.
PENELOPE: He's gone. Who is responsible for this monstrous and devious act? How are we supposed to carry on now?

AUNTIE SOPHIE *enters.*

SOPHIE: Oh my Lord! What has happened to Frederick?
BENJAMIN: I'm so sorry to tell you this, Auntie Sophie, but Father has been stabbed to death.
SOPHIE: What! This is a safe and secure mansion. How could this possibly happen? My brother can't leave me like this. I feel so dizzy all of a sudden and very sick. (*She becomes upset.*) I never thought I would live to see this day. I have to go and lie down.

AUNTIE SOPHIE *exits.*

BENJAMIN: Penchard, call the local authorities immediately. We need urgent attention.
PENCHARD: He was going to do the main oration. He had spent so much time on the speech this year.
PENELOPE: Penchard, you miserable twit! Father's life has been snatched by some dangerous villain and all you can think about is the Dex!
PENCHARD: Nobody seems to be picking up.
BENJAMIN: What the hell are you going on about now? Give me that phone. You're absolutely useless. (*He puts the receiver to his ear.*) I don't believe this. The phone's dead. There's no dialling tone.
PENELOPE: This is the worst day of my life!
PENCHARD: I'll go and check the phone next door.

PENCHARD *exits.*

BENJAMIN: This person has calculated everything to the last detail.
PENELOPE: Why is the back door unlocked? I locked that door when I came back in. Or did I? I can't remember. Oh my God, I'm responsible for Father's death. I let the murderer

in. I let him kill Father. I should have checked the handle before I left the room. Ben, this is all my fault, isn't it?
BENJAMIN: Now, now, Penny. (*Benjamin comforts her*.) You must not get hysterical. This is not your fault at all.
PENELOPE: But I should have checked. I can't help thinking that had the door been locked the killer would have thought twice.

PENCHARD *returns*.

PENCHARD: I'm afraid all the telephone lines have been destroyed. I've sent Coral and Meesha out to inform the local authorities. The security staff will look after Mr Devereux until they arrive with the police.
BENJAMIN: Thank you. I still can't take all this in.
PENCHARD: Master Benjamin, everything is going to fall apart now. Life without the master will certainly be miserable and hopeless. I depended upon him for all wisdom and direction. Now that has all gone.
BENJAMIN: We'd better inform the crowd. Sadly we have arrived at the end of a remarkable era with unexpected brutal bloodshed.
PENCHARD: Yes. Yes. We should. But I feel so shaky.
BENJAMIN: Calm your nerves, Penchard! We all need to be strong. Now let's go. Come on Penny. We have to do this.
PENCHARD: Yes. Let's try and focus. (*He takes a deep breath*.) Dear Lord, may you rest his soul in peace. May the guilty party be punished for this crime. Please help and guide us through this difficult time. Amen.
BENJAMIN & PENELOPE: Amen.

They all exit.

SCENE TWENTY-THREE

The following week. SOPHIE, BENJAMIN, THOMAS *and* VERONICA *are all gathered in the front room. Everyone is sitting in cold silence looking away from one another.*

BENJAMIN: What kind of father arranges his son's wedding without telling him?
THOMAS: Whose wedding? What wedding?
SOPHIE: I knew it wasn't a good idea from the very beginning. Your father just wouldn't listen to me.
BENJAMIN: What a charming and caring parent I had!
VERONICA: (*very distressed*) If anyone wishes to speak ill of Frederick then please leave this room now. I will not have this kind of horrible talk straight after his demise.
THOMAS: This is the worst possible thing that could have happened.
SOPHIE: Absolutely awful!
THOMAS: I just hope that he does not start harassing my mother. She is happy as she is at the moment. We had a nice long chat the day before yesterday.
SOPHIE: Why during the Dex? Why did this have to happen?
VERONICA: You do realise that we are all under suspicion? The authorities have got their eyes on us as well as others.
BENJAMIN: I certainly had nothing to do with it. I would never dream of such a thing!
THOMAS: I definitely didn't do it. I was so drunk I couldn't even stand up properly.
BENJAMIN: Great! All under suspicion for murder. What a wonderful end to the week!
VERONICA: So did any of you think about killing him?

SOPHIE: What an absurd thing to say, Veronica! We are his family. We would not under any circumstances want to kill him! Of course there were moments of anger and many disagreements, but no one could have imagined murdering him.
VERONICA: Shoes. Those shoes.
BENJAMIN: Mother, what are you talking about?
VERONICA: Shoes. Just those shoes. I have seen them before.
THOMAS: Sounds like a song!
VERONICA: It's not a song. It is real.
BENJAMIN: Mother, what shoes?
VERONICA: Those shoes are the reason it happened. I know. Those shoes are the cause of all this.
SOPHIE: What are you gabbling on about? Sounds like you're going mad!
VERONICA: I am not mad. I am right.
SOPHIE: There were so many guests, how on earth are they going to conclude their investigation? It could have been anybody. He did make a lot of enemies, after all.
VERONICA: Yes. We know that. But half of them were superficial. Only of the moment. We need to look further than that. It must be someone of prominent significance who holds a tremendous grudge.
SOPHIE: Yes, but who?
VERONICA: I need to go for a walk. Clear my mind a little bit. Ben, do you want to come?
BENJAMIN: Of course I'll come with you. I'll go and fetch my coat.

VERONICA *and* BENJAMIN *exit.*

THOMAS: So did you do it, Auntie Sophie? Did you kill my father with a great big grin?
SOPHIE: What a preposterous thing to say! He is your father and my brother. I would not do such a thing. I have far more dignity than that.

THOMAS: I understand what you are saying, but it could be true, couldn't it? I mean, with all due respect, maybe past history triggered this type of bloody action.
SOPHIE: Thomas, please leave the questions to the experts.
THOMAS: Well, I want to be a serious part of this investigation. I want to do some police work.
SOPHIE: You are part of this investigation. You are one of the apparent suspects. You never really liked your father, did you?
THOMAS: So? What has that got to do with it?
SOPHIE: When the inspectors hear of your father and son relationship, I am sure they will dart over here to probe you further.
THOMAS: If I were the killer I wouldn't have stabbed him to death. I would have poisoned him. He would sit at the dining table, consume the main course and then, boom, the fantastic desert. Nothing like a great caramel surprise!
SOPHIE: I see. Well, if I were of that malicious mind I would have taken him far away and discreetly silenced him.
THOMAS: You mean, you would have used some sort of crowbar or a long sharp poker?
SOPHIE: Perhaps.
THOMAS: Aren't we supposed to be sad now that Father has passed away?
SOPHIE: Yes. That is the inevitable consequence.
THOMAS: So how come I don't feel any sadness? I just want to go and have a drink and warn Mother that the man who had made her life hell in this world, is now coming to meet her. I am very concerned about her safety and well-being.
SOPHIE: Why would Frederick be meeting up with Loni anyway? Frederick is going straight to hell. Loni is not there. Loni's characteristics are far from cruelty, arrogance and selfishness. She was a wonderful human being.
THOMAS: My mother was the best. Until he killed her. My father was a vicious murderer. So he deserved to be killed. I am glad

his death was not peaceful. I hate him. I have always hated him. He never was the father that I had been searching for. He was too nasty towards me. I hope God is merciless. I am not going to the dreary funeral wearing a hypocrite's badge.

SOPHIE: Now, now! No matter what, he was your father. You should not talk like that.

THOMAS: But it is the truth. He took my mother away from me. I love her more than anyone else in this mansion. I worship her. (*He stands up and raises his voice.*) Frederick Charles Devereux, if you are listening to me now, then here is what I have to say to you. You will see no painful tears from my depressing eyes. You will never see me experience any grief-stricken heartache due to your unexpected demise. I am not going to remember you. You treated me like a worthless piece of rubbish! You treated me like dirt! You had no respect for me and you loathed the sight of me. I too have learnt to reciprocate. I have hated you for a very long time. This glorious news only hails a new beginning for us all here in Fezaria-Aston. Let us hope and pray that everyone around here forgets about you and that they will join us to consecrate your holy arrival into hell. You dare approach my mother. When it is my turn I will not think twice about assassinating you. You hear me loud and clear? You leave my mother alone. You leave her in peace. She will not save you from any harm. For you, there is no life after death. It is simply indefatigable torture. You will no doubt appreciate and savour every moment of it. Farewell, Father. May you rest in pain forever.

SOPHIE: Thomas, calm down.

THOMAS: The cold-hearted tyrant is dead. We must celebrate, Auntie.

SOPHIE: Thomas, when the media appear before us, please do not voice this sort of discourse. They will not understand your true feelings and instead they will assist the locals in isolating you as the murderer.

THOMAS: Yes, I am aware that is a possibility, but can they prove anything? Of course not! Therefore I am out of harm's way.
SOPHIE: Poor Nancy! She has already cried a flood of tears.
THOMAS: I think you will find her to be the only one with any honest tears. The rest of us are gratefully breathing a sigh of relief. Auntie Sophie, are you ready?
SOPHIE: For what?
THOMAS: I am going out to celebrate. Would you care to join me?
SOPHIE: You must refrain from showing your true sentiments.
THOMAS: Very well, then. You go and pretend whilst I celebrate until the early hours of the morning. Good day to you.
SOPHIE: Thomas, please be careful what you say in front of other people.
THOMAS: I will only be drinking. With lots of ice.

THOMAS *joyfully exits.*

SCENE TWENTY-FOUR

PENELOPE *is comforting* NANCY. PENCHARD *is sitting in* FREDERICK's *armchair. He remains totally bemused.* PETER *enters.*

PETER: Would anyone like a cup of tea? Or anything else?
PENCHARD: No thank you, Peter! Please leave us alone.
PETER: May I ask, are there any new leads on the murder? Any new evidence?
PENCHARD: Why? What do you know?
PETER: I was just concerned, that's all.
PENCHARD: Did you kill him?
PETER: No. No. Of course not! Why would I do that?
PENCHARD: Revenge.
PETER: Revenge? How ridiculous!
PENCHARD: Do you know something that I don't, Peter? Or any of the other staff?
PETER: Why are you trying to accuse us? We never intended to kill him. We would never think of murdering our employer! Do you think we would really get away with it? Besides I thought they had found their culprit?
PENELOPE: They've only taken him in for interrogation. Nothing more.
PENCHARD: Hopefully, they will find the miserable perpetrator and punish him until he dies a gloomy and painful death.
PENELOPE: Daniel would never kill Father. He was too scared of him in the first place.
PENCHARD: There are many ways of looking at it.

PENELOPE: Daniel is innocent. They will not be able to lay a finger on him.

PENCHARD: I still cannot believe that he has gone. His last affable words to me were 'I hope the Dex is as successful as last year, Penchard. Let us go and throw open the doors and enjoy the essence of enthralling wealth.' Everything was running perfectly. Every single detail was in delightful order. There were no silly setbacks. That must have been an omen. Normally, something does go wrong. Jack Haddy was so distraught.

PENELOPE: He has been taken in for questioning as well, hasn't he?

PENCHARD: That is simply a minor hindrance. We all know that Jack Haddy lives and breathes for Frederick Devereux, the supreme sire. There is absolutely no genuine reason why he should be the offender.

PENELOPE: You may be surprised!

PENCHARD: It could be Braswick. He was so irate about losing his position at one of the Devereux factories. He did promise to get even.

PENELOPE: I do not think getting even means killing his former employer. That would not make any sense.

NANCY: It's got to be the depraved and disloyal Veronica! The argumentative bitch never did support my father in anything he did. She was seldom pleasant and understanding towards him.

PENELOPE: No. It can't be her. She's not that clever!

NANCY: You do not need to be a genius to murder someone. You just need courage.

PENELOPE: It isn't her. It's not Daniel, for sure. It's somebody else.

NANCY: Veronica is responsible. Nobody else. I hated her from the first moment I saw her. She may seem polite on the outside but on the inside she breeds filthy contempt and ruthless conspiracy. I know her very well. She may show

deep sorrow and pretend to cry an ocean of tears but she is the one to blame.
PENELOPE: I simply believe it was an outsider. Nobody, especially family, would perform such a callous act.
PETER: So nobody wants a drink?
PENCHARD: Just get out, you thoughtless and defiant boy.
PETER: Only doing my job!

He exits in an exasperated manner.

NANCY: I have to sell the shop. I have to move away from Fezaria-Aston. Every corner I turn will remind me of these awful hours. My father has left me. How could I possibly carry on? My father believed in me so much. I loved him dearly and I still do. I miss him. When I think about how much pain he was in, it truly wounds me. I feel so hurt and so lonely.
PENELOPE: I know. I know. We shall all miss him.
NANCY: If I find out that it was Veronica I will strangle her to death. I will enjoy every minute of it.
PENCHARD: Ms Devereux, you must be patient. The person responsible for this cannot run far. He will perish too.
PENELOPE: How do you know it's a man?
PENCHARD: Because only a man would know how to stab his prey repeatedly. A woman can only stab once or twice.
NANCY: That's not true.
PENELOPE: Why wouldn't a woman know how to stab repeatedly?
PENCHARD: Because a woman can easily get distracted or nervous. You need more than a few seconds to use a knife in anger.
NANCY: Now you're talking nonsense.

Suddenly there is a knock at the door. MEESHA *enters with a large bouquet of flowers.*

MEESHA: Sorry to interrupt, but these arrived for you, Ms Devereux.
NANCY: For Me? (*taking the bouquet and putting them on the table*)
MEESHA: The florist just delivered them. I think there's a small note.
NANCY: (*She takes the little envelope and opens it up.*) 'What a surprising end in history! You have lost! Now where is the money? Kindest Regards Angela and Crane.' What is this? Meesha, is this some kind of sick joke?
MEESHA: Ms Devereux, I wouldn't dream of it in light of what has happened!
NANCY: Who on earth are Angela and Crane?
MEESHA: I honestly do not know!
PENCHARD: We are here, suffering unspeakable misery, and the menaces of society are choosing to make fun of us. How dare they, how dare they!
MEESHA: Ms Devereux, please believe me, I have absolutely no idea who these people are. I would never do anything harmful towards your family. Ever! I am truly sorry for our loss.
NANCY: Dispose of these flowers at once. I demand you take them now and burn them! Go on, hurry up.

MEESHA *hurriedly takes them and exits.*

PENELOPE: What a disgusting gesture, to say the least.
NANCY: This is what it's going to be like. This is what people are going to do.
PENELOPE: Aren't Angela and Crane acquaintances of yours or something?
NANCY: To suggest such a ridiculous thing makes you even more stupid. How dare you!
PENCHARD: I wish he were alive today. I feel completely lost without his guidance. Wherever you are, Mr Devereux, I

hope you are well. I miss you awfully, kind sir. I am always thinking of you. Please protect me as each day goes by.
NANCY: Now, if you wouldn't mind, please could I be left alone. I need time to myself. I need time to grieve.
PENELOPE: Would you like me to stay with you?
NANCY: No, that is all right. I just want to be on my own now. Thank you.

As PENELOPE *and* PENCHARD *exit,* NANCY *quickly jumps up from her seat and telephones someone.*

NANCY: Hello, Crane?
CRANE: (*offstage*) The final call before dawn. What can I do for you?
NANCY: What are you up to? Where are those access codes?
CRANE: What a terrible state of affairs you are facing. I thought you would be grateful for the touching gesture.
NANCY: It wasn't amusing.
CRANE: I was only being polite. Or should I say, Angela thought it would be courteous to send you a reminder about our deal.
NANCY: Crane, where are the access codes?
CRANE: Well, they were in my pocket only a few moments ago, but when I last had a peek they were gone. Oh dear!
NANCY: Crane, now is not the time for jokes!
CRANE: I am not one for jesting. Those codes have disappeared.
NANCY: Are you serious?
CRANE: Yes. I am one hundred percent serious. I no longer have those precious codes. After hearing what happened, I sold them.
NANCY: What?!
CRANE: I sold them for a very good juicy, mouth-watering cut.
NANCY: You traitor! You bloody traitor! I will get you for this.

CRANE: Angela says hi! Mishty is still packing her case. She is so sorry about what happened to your father. Pity somebody beat you to it. We'll be off to Acapulco in the next few hours. Give our love to the rest of your family.
NANCY: Wait! Wait! To whom did you sell those codes?
CRANE: I was sworn to secrecy.
NANCY: Crane, who is it?
CRANE: Oh, what the hell! It was that ugly-looking guy that works for your father. What's his name again? Let me think. Pritchard? Pollard? Pen ... Penchard! Your father's faithful slave. Goodbye, Nancy. Hope you keep well.
NANCY: How much did he pay you?
CRANE: I can only smell lovely roses now and sweet air.
NANCY: How much, you fool?
CRANE: We have £50 million now. I could just sit and eat every single bit of it. I am rich and you are now destitute. If you ever need me I'll eventually be at Comaha. Please feel free to send a pigeon!

CRANE *hangs up and* NANCY*'s rage induces screaming.*

SCENE TWENTY-FIVE

AUNTIE SOPHIE *is in a luxurious hotel room. She is holding up a glass of wine celebrating with a female companion of similar age and stature.*

SOPHIE: Here's a toast to the best outcome ever! May we prosper and live wonderful lives.
LONI: Here! Here! We certainly did well, didn't we? Just thinking about it feels so amazing. I just can't believe it. I had such an adrenalin rush. My heart was palpitating madly.
SOPHIE: But you have succeeded. You are definitely more courageous than I am. I am truly impressed. If this objective had been placed on my shoulders, I would have felt so nervous and sick.
LONI: Two heads are always better than one, and our plan was triumphant. I couldn't have done it without your continuous support. Now it's over. We can begin to live a normal life. For the very first time, I'll get to see, talk and spend time with my children.
SOPHIE: Did you finally decide to tell Vanessa about our worthy scheme?
LONI: I informed Vanessa that very soon she will be meeting the rest of her family. She was very excited to hear that. She's only seen pictures of them.
SOPHIE: I'm looking forward to it as well. It's going to be a tremendous day. Thomas, Nancy, Penelope and Vanessa, you and I, altogether at one table, sitting, laughing and enjoying each other's company. It seems like a miracle.
LONI: I did do the right thing by never telling Frederick about Vanessa, didn't I?

SOPHIE: Oh absolutely! If he didn't care about you, then why would he have shown concern for your unborn child?

LONI: The bastard ruined my life. He completely destroyed me. Physically and mentally.

SOPHIE: I remember it as if it were yesterday. Your dreary funeral, the unrecognisable dead body, your tasteless obituary and your fictitious wake. All meticulously carried out and very convincing. I was in shock. (*Pause*) I had just returned from Bridgenorth. There was such a morose atmosphere within the mansion. Nancy and Penelope were sobbing their eyes out. Thomas had a blank look on his face. He was sitting with one of the maids in total silence. Cook approached me. She was very upset. She told me the awful news. Apparently, you had taken an overdose and slipped down the staircase. Frederick was on the telephone at the time. I distinctly recall him saying 'Don't worry, we can make this work.' The moment he spotted me he hung up, changed his facial expression and addressed me very sadly. He pretended to break down in tears. Naturally I was sympathetic. To think I held Frederick in my arms to console him when the whole appalling masquerade was his doing.

LONI: He told me to leave Fezaria-Aston very quietly. And never to come back. My only fault was that I had told him how I felt so lonely and how a recent friendship with a male acquaintance had helped me get through my solitude. Suddenly there was a stupid and meaningless rumour going around.

SOPHIE: Yes. I remember that too. Something about you and Michael Bishop being a keen and happy couple.

LONI: He was a shoulder to cry on. Someone to talk to and understand my feelings. He always appreciated how hard it was with young children, especially without a proper father figure.

SOPHIE: Then one day, as the rumour got out of hand, I bumped into one of his crude associates in the main hall. He had arrived to express his concern and utter disapproval about what was going on. That man was in there for hours. Frederick was uncontrollably angry.

LONI: Unfortunately, Michael Bishop turned out to be an ex-employee who had been fired for stealing company property.

SOPHIE: But wasn't he framed?

LONI: Yes, he was framed by Penchard, but he left without saying a word. He decided not to talk about it. He became depressed after that.

SOPHIE: When Frederick found out that Michael was a past employee whom he had kicked out, he was extremely angry.

LONI: So angry that he decided to totally ruin my life. Twenty-six years of it. The day I left without my children, was the day I died inside. I became absolutely numb. I never had the power to do anything really. He didn't even give me a chance to explain. He rudely confronted me. As he yelled the house down, he pointed at me vigorously. He abused me and swore at me. Then I was ordered to leave immediately. As I cried, I went to pack some of my belongings, but he followed me and dragged me out of the bedroom and disgracefully pushed me out. Before slamming the door in my face, he threw me a five-pound note. His last words were 'Five pounds should be adequate for your needs.' He didn't even allow me to see my children. He said an unfaithful tramp has no children, only the road in front of her.

SOPHIE: The staff were summoned and informed that you had been admitted into hospital with severe injuries sustained, after falling down the stairs. He accused you of having depression and proving to be an unfit mother. He described you as abusive and frosty towards the children and as a wife a regrettable mistake. He stressed how unhappy he was to have had the ill fortune of meeting you. He mimicked a heartbroken and lonely husband. Some of the staff were quite unsure about the entire story. At that time my main worries were for the children, especially Thomas.

LONI: That week whilst I was at my parents a long stern anonymous letter arrived. It was a heavily descriptive explanation of how my life would be dictated for the rest of my years alive, and how I would never be allowed to alter any aspect of it. There were numerous threats. I was deeply saddened by his poisonous language and the repetition of 'You will perish a ghastly death if you in any way disagree.' I wept and wept. My dramatic demise not only complicated my whole life but hurt me ceaselessly. He exclaimed that he would be doing me an immense favour by rubbing my face out of society. My parents could not believe it either. My world had fallen apart because of one cruel, vindictive and unreasonable human being.

SOPHIE: Thomas has never recovered from the loss. He misses you every minute of every day. He still speaks to you at the cemetery. He chats to you about many things and when he becomes isolated he begins to drink until he cannot drink anymore.

LONI: After I had calmed down, I thought to myself that enough was enough. So I decided to go back to the mansion and stand my ground. Sadly, security came hurling after me. I then realised the restraining order was true. The next day another anonymous note appeared, this time ordering me to leave my own home town for good and never to show my face again, as my funeral was in a few weeks time. With so many violent and derogatory comments, I seriously had to choose. Should I fight or should I give up?

SOPHIE: My unsettled mind could not really believe that you were dead. It was too mechanical. So I decided to investigate. As I persevered, one of the locals was able to point me in the right direction. I just knew my suspicions were true.

LONI: I was so happy and relieved when you came to visit me. The long and tedious hours at the paper mill were wearing me out.

SOPHIE: Your parents were so delighted to hear that you were fit and well.
LONI: With your kind help and absolute support, once more I had plucked up the courage to confront Frederick, but my confidence was thoroughly shattered by the announcement of his second marriage.
SOPHIE: I still stand by my judgement. According to Frederick, Veronica was chosen to fill a gap. He began to crack under pressure. After meeting Veronica, he had words with her family and friends and within three weeks of meeting her he had proposed a quiet wedding ceremony. Only immediate family were invited. I refused to attend, but Frederick forced me. I absolutely hated Veronica and I still do.
LONI: He married so quickly. He evidently was too eager to replace me. I suppose we never really loved each other. We only married because it seemed like a great idea at the time.
SOPHIE: But you have four lovely children out of it. Even though the circumstances were not so superb.
LONI: Yes! Of course. All those pictures that you sent reminded me that I was never alone. They were fabulous photographs. I cannot believe how quickly Thomas grew up. Penelope still has her baby face and Nancy looks too much like her father. I have missed so much. When I see them again I'm just going to cry and cry. There will be no words to make up for the past twenty-six years. Except heartfelt regret and ponderous guilt.
SOPHIE: Now, let us put all that misery and struggle behind us and look forward to the new.
LONI: Absolutely!

There is a hard knock at the door. SOPHIE *rises cautiously.*

SOPHIE: Do you think that is him?
LONI: I think so. He's on time, as you requested.

SOPHIE: I'm so nervous all of a sudden.
LONI: Be calm. Go and open the door. Don't keep the poor boy waiting.

She slowly opens the door. A member of the mansion staff appears. The tall figure turns round.

SOPHIE: Peter! I'm so glad you came.
PETER: Ms Devereux, I received your note. You said that it was urgent and you wished to tell me something important. You mentioned a reunion?
LONI: Good luck.

LONI *picks up her bag and puts on her hat. She smiles at* PETER *and then exits.*

Sophie: Come in, Peter. I have many things to discuss with you. At last.

PETER *nervously walks in.*

SCENE TWENTY-SIX – DENOUEMENT

LONI *descends to the fountain gardens of the hotel. She walks until a wooden bench appears. She sits down, gazes into the sky and begins to think deeply.*

LONI: My prison sentence is over at last! I have found myself once more. Committing suicide would have definitely been the wrong thing to do. My children would have, no doubt, cursed me. I am a proud murderer. I am thoroughly delighted. I have no regrets. The sheer idea of Frederick being alive has always threatened my well-being and my children's. Now I stand victorious but I have blood on my hands. Will this ever go? Nevertheless, my stained hands have released me. My freedom awaits my arrival. But am I ready for this? All these years I have been enduring frustration and hatred. Now that frustration and hatred have disappeared. So what exactly do I feel now? What if my children hate me? Will they question my courage, my beliefs and, above all, will they interrogate me too much about the past? I do not wish to build my future with remnants of the past. I know for certain that Thomas will hate me the most. I fear his judgement. I fear his tone. How would I begin to address him and the rest? I realise Sophie has cautioned me not to reveal our secret, but what if they find out? No, no, what am I thinking? It's not possible. Nobody saw me. The disguise was too complicated. The weapon was hidden. I have succeeded. There is nothing further to worry about. There will be no stormy comeback. (*Pause*) For the first time I can hear the birds singing. I can feel the clear breeze. I can enjoy the sunshine. Now I can look forward to being a part of everyday life. But what about guilt? Do I actually feel any guilt? Do I feel remorse? Why should I? Frederick made my life hell. He destroyed me. So of course there should be no self-reproach. I did what any woman would have done in my shoes. I have a right to live. I have a right to my freedom. Oh no, but it is bloodstained freedom. Surely I deserve better? Surely I deserve to be free? I refuse to see myself as a murderer. I had no choice but to kill him. Oh God, what have I done?! When I meet my children for the first time it will be in the guise of a murderer. I have committed a crime. But wait a minute. It was all provoked. This was not an intentional conspiracy. This was all the product of his wickedness towards me. He is the one to blame. What will Thomas say or think once he finds out? I cannot bear to think about it. Nancy might look at me with evil eyes. Penelope will be disgusted and Vanessa will be traumatised. Having just reunited with my family I will lose them again because of my dark secret. They will resent me and here I am preparing to meet them with a criminal's face. Criminal. Criminal. Criminal. No. No. No. I didn't want this. I have never wanted this. I have been blessed with four lovely children. As a mother I was denied the wealth of happiness. Now I have the grand opportunity of making amends, but with bloodstained hands. Bloodstained! Bloodstained! What is on your hands? Blood. Frederick's blood. A tyrant's blood. The father of my children's blood. My husband's blood. Blackened hands. Cruel hands. Poor Veronica! She must be devastated. I feel sorry for her. I wonder if she will miss him. The problem I have now is what am I going to say to Reece? He loves Vanessa dearly, as if she were his own daughter. To tell him about her siblings may threaten our relationship. I do hope not. What if he finds out that I murdered Frederick? Will he still look at me the same way as before? My defence is mental and physical provocation. But was killing Frederick a wise idea? Maybe Sophie should have stabbed him? I am sure Sophie wouldn't have felt so much guilt.

A shadow grows from behind. The mysterious figure taps her on the shoulder. LONI *rises as she turns around.*

VERONICA: It was you, wasn't it?
LONI: Veronica? How did you ...
VERONICA: I followed you. You placed the red ribbon under the door. That was your signal. You were the anonymous guest who knew her way around the mansion. Your choice of footwear hasn't changed and you are wearing the same wedding ring.
LONI: I am truly sorry.
VERONICA: Thank you for making me a widow. You have killed the root of all evil. May God bless you!

VERONICA *smiles and then gives* LONI *a delicate hug.*